Concise Guide to
Information Literacy

Obviously, a man's judgment cannot be better than the information on which he has based it.

Arthur Hays Sulzberger
Publisher of *The New York Times* from 1935 to 1961

Knowing a great deal is not the same as being smart; intelligence is not information alone but also judgment, the manner in which information is collected and used.

Carl Sagan
Astrophysicist and writer

Concise Guide to Information Literacy

Second Edition

Scott Lanning

 LIBRARIES
UNLIMITED™

An Imprint of ABC-CLIO, LLC

Santa Barbara, California • Denver, Colorado

Library of Congress Cataloging-in-Publication Data

Names: Lanning, Scott, author.
Title: Concise guide to information literacy / Scott Lanning.
Description: Second edition. | Santa Barbara, California : Libraries Unlimited, an
    imprint of ABC-CLIO, LLC, [2017] | Includes bibliographical references and index.
Identifiers: LCCN 2016056351 (print) | LCCN 2017006849 (ebook) |
    ISBN 9781440851384 (paperback : acid-free paper) | ISBN 9781440851391 (ebook)
Subjects: LCSH: Information literacy—Handbooks, manuals, etc. | Information retrieval—
    Handbooks, manuals, etc. | Research—Methodology—Handbooks, manuals, etc. |
    Report writing—Handbooks, manuals, etc.
Classification: LCC ZA3075 .L36 2017 (print) | LCC ZA3075 (ebook) | DDC 028.7—dc23
LC record available at https://lccn.loc.gov/2016056351

ISBN: 978-1-4408-5138-4
EISBN: 978-1-4408-5139-1

21 20 19   3 4 5

This book is also available as an eBook.

Libraries Unlimited
An Imprint of ABC-CLIO, LLC

ABC-CLIO, LLC
130 Cremona Drive, P.O. Box 1911
Santa Barbara, California 93116-1911
www.abc-clio.com

This book is printed on acid-free paper ∞

Manufactured in the United States of America

To my best friend, and biggest fan—my beautiful wife.

Contents

List of Figures

Information and Information Literacy

In This Chapter

You will learn:

- What this book is about
- What literate means
- What information is
- What information literacy is
- Why information literacy is important

Jargon and the Study of Disciplines

This book is full of jargon. Jargon is the language of a discipline. In this case, the jargon in this book concerns information literacy. Every discipline has its own vocabulary, its jargon. The jargon of biology is different from that of chemistry, sociology, psychology, math, and history. Understanding the language will help you understand the discipline.

This book will give you an understanding of the special language of information literacy and try to teach you some of the fundamental concepts of the discipline with the intent of giving you enough skills to participate successfully in the information world, and enjoy all the benefits that being information literate entails in the world at large and as your information skills continue to grow.

What Does It Mean to Be Literate?

We all have a basic understanding of what it means to be literate. When we say someone is literate, we usually mean that that person can read and write. If someone is illiterate, he or she is lacking in one or both of those skills. This is indeed one of the meanings of literate.

However, there is a much broader and older definition of literate. According to the *Oxford English Dictionary*, a literate person is an educated person ("Literate" 2016). This meaning of literate dates to about A.D. 1475. So what does it mean to be educated? In A.D. 1475, it meant being able to read and write. What does it mean to be educated, today? We have more information, more technology, and more ways to communicate it than anyone from the Middle Ages could have dreamed. We need to know more than just how to read and write to be literate.

What Are Some of the Literacies?

We need a wide range of discipline-specific literacies to be educated. We need:

Visual literacy

Digital literacy

Financial literacy

Geographic literacy

Cultural literacy

Media literacy

Scientific literacy

Digital life literacy

Health literacy

Computer literacy

Historical literacy

STEM literacy

Data literacy

Metaliteracy

Civic literacy

Economic literacy

Multicultural literacy

Global literacy

Critical literacy

Information literacy

Don't be intimidated by this partial list of literacies. You don't need to be an economist to be economically literate. You need to know enough about economics to understand the impact local, national, and world economic issues have on you and others.

You need to understand that some of these literacies overlap each other. For example, being economically literate will help you with your global literacy. However, the concept of global literacy encompasses much more than just economics, including civics, sociology, labor, and the environment among other topics.

The focus of this book is information literacy, and it includes aspects of data, digital, civic, media, visual, and other literacies. We will get to all of these in one form or another in this book, but right now, we need to start with the basics.

What Is Information?

We looked at literacy. Now we will examine information. Information is defined as:

> Data which has been recorded, classified, organized, related, or interpreted within a framework so that meaning emerges. ("Information" 2003)

Information can take many forms. It can be words on a page, charts, tables, graphs (Figure 1.1), pictures, audio, and video. Is the following information?

- 36070

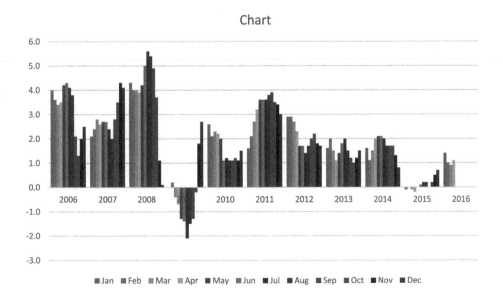

Figure 1.1: Undefined Chart

No. Neither of these is information. They are data. They need some kind of context for their meaning to be discerned. In the first case, we have a number and no idea what it means beyond its numerical value. We can rewrite the number as 36,070 ft. Now we know it is a measure of something. If we place this measurement in the Pacific Ocean, then you would be right in saying this is the depth of the Mariana Trench ("Mariana Trench" 2016).

In the case of the chart, if we add more information to it to give it a context from which it can be understood, it would look like this (Figure 1.2).

Now our chart makes more sense. It is the rate of inflation in the United States for the past 10+ years by month ("Bureau of Labor Statistics Data" 2016). Now both of these are examples of information.

Not only are there many forms that information can take, but there are also many sources of information. Information can come from traditional sources like news outlets, which may be a television broadcast, a Website, or a magazine. Information can be discovered, and uncovered. The scientists at CERN who discover new subatomic particles, and pass that information on to us, have created new information. The researcher who finds a medicinal use for a plant from the South American rain forests, and published her findings has created information. You will create information every time your write a paper.

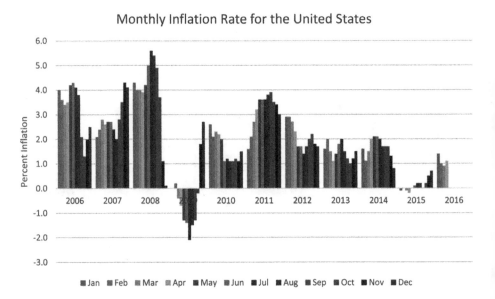

Figure 1.2: Defined Chart

Information comes from your teachers in class, and your friends after class. Information does not have to be about big happenings in the world. It can be that tweet you sent about the unidentifiable food you just ate for lunch, or it can be the show times of the new movie you want to see.

What Is Information Literacy?

Now that we have an understanding of what information and literacy mean, we turn our attention to information literacy. Information literacy is the ability to recognize an information need, find, evaluate, manage, synthesize, use, and communicate information efficiently, effectively, and ethically to answer that information need. This requires knowledge of the tools used in the process. Since most materials are found and/or used in an electronic format, you need digital literacy skills, like using computers and software to find, store, and use information. You need knowledge of resources and research tools, and a basic understanding of the publishing process, and what that means to the quality of the information you found. You need critical skills to evaluate not only the information you found, but also to reflect upon what you have done at each step of the process, and where you could do better next time.

An information need can be anything from determining a fair price for a good used car to developing a new product. Writing a research paper involves a number of information literacy processes, like finding and using information to answer your research question, and support or disprove your hypothesis. To do this well, you will need to evaluate the information you use to ensure its quality while synthesizing that information in order to draw your own conclusions. You will need to manage that information so you can refer to it as you are writing and give credit to the authors whose information and ideas you use in your paper.

We will examine in more detail each piece of the definition of information literacy in future chapters. Right now, there is one more question to answer in this chapter, and it is perhaps the most import question in the book.

Why Is Information Literacy Important?

There are many reasons that information literacy is important. However, you should be skeptical when a librarian tells you that it is important because it is such an important part of what we do. We believe information literacy is a vital skill. It overlaps with all subject areas and disciplines (see Figure 1.3). You need to be information literate to be a writer, a chemist, and a successful student.

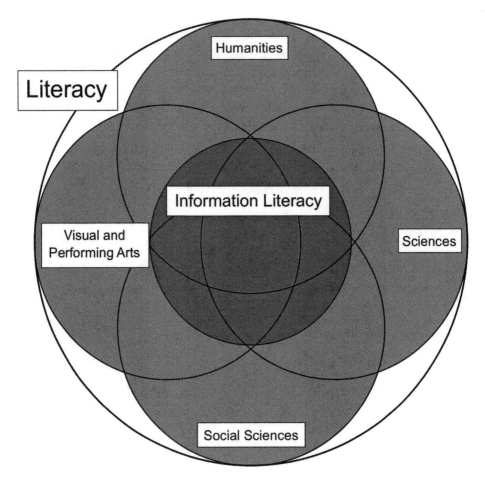

Figure 1.3: The Relationship between the Literacies

However, many other organizations feel the same way. The organizations that accredit colleges and universities, that recognize when a college meets a certain standard of quality, believe that information literacy is important. The Middle States Association of Colleges and Schools says that colleges should offer a curriculum "designed so that students acquire and demonstrate essential skills including at least oral and written communication, scientific and quantitative reasoning, critical analysis and reasoning, technological competency, and information literacy" (Middle States Commission on Higher Education 2014). The New England Association of Schools and Colleges states that students who graduate with an undergraduate degree should "demonstrate competence in written and oral communication in English; the ability for scientific and quantitative reasoning, for critical analysis and logical thinking; and the capability for continuing learning, including the skills of information literacy" ("Standards [Effective July 1, 2016]" 2016).

Accrediting agencies are not the only ones concerned with information literacy. *The Prague Declaration* came from a United Nations Educational, Scientific and Cultural Organization (UNESCO)–supported conference with the National Forum on Information Literacy (http://infolit.org), a not-for-profit organization with and international membership dedicated to promoting information literacy, and the National Commission on Libraries and Information Science which is a U.S. government agency now called the Institute of Museum and Library Services (http://www.imls.gov). The conference had representatives from 23 countries who agreed that the "creation of an Information Society is key to social, cultural and economic development of nations and communities, institutions and individuals" and that information literacy is "a prerequisite for participating effectively in the Information Society, and is part of the basic human right to life long learning." They also stated information literacy reduces inequities and promotes tolerance and understanding. They concluded by saying that governments around the world should develop strong programs to promote information literacy to create and "information literate citizenry, an effective civil society and a competitive workforce" (UNESCO 2003).

Librarians do have something to say on the matter. The American Association of School Librarians (AASL), an important and influential organization of librarians, in its *Standards for the 21st-Century Learner,* lists a number of reasons why information literacy is important, including the ability to make informed decisions, create new knowledge, pursue personal growth, and participate, both ethically and productively, in our democratic society (American Association of School Librarians 2007).

If you need more practical reasons why information literacy is important, then look to the business world. A research study found that information literacy abilities are closely related to workplace functions like environmental scanning, information management, and research and development (Bruce 1999, 34). Another study points out that the business world requires employees to be able to create, package, and present information effectively to a specific audience. In other words, it is a set of abilities that enable employees to work with information when they need to examine business issues and problems (Cheuk 2008, 139). The problem is that employees abandon 50% of their searches, and when writing reports, spend up to 90% of their time re-creating reports that already exist. This inefficiency costs businesses in the United States more than $100 billion per year (Birdsong and Freitas 2012, 593)! Finally, companies that invest in training their employees, a lifelong learning activity that information literacy abilities make more effective, return more money to their shareholders (O'Sullivan 2002, 8).

If all of the above are not enough reasons why information literacy is important, then consider the following two quotes. Richard Dawkins, a prominent evolutionary biologist, said, "What lies at the heart of every living thing is not a fire, not warm breath, not a 'spark of life'. It is information, words, instructions" (1986, 112). James Gleick, a Pulitzer Prize–nominated author, stated in his book *The Information: A History, a Theory, a Flood*, "Information is what our world runs on: the blood and the fuel, the vital principle" (2011, 8). We are creatures of information, built by information, powered by information, consuming and producing information. Shouldn't we know what information is and how to sift through the billions of bits of information to find the pieces we need? We must be able to live well in our information society, and that requires information literacy.

Vocabulary

creation of information
data
forms of information
information
information literacy
information need
jargon
lifelong learning
literate
sources of information

Questions for Reflection

Where does information come from?
What information have you created in the past week?
What does it mean to participate in our democratic society?
What is a "global citizen"?
Why is lifelong learning important?

Assignment

You will start by creating a research journal to track the work you do for this class.

For your first entry, pick two of the literacies listed in this chapter and/or find one of your own, and find two definitions of each from the

Internet (Figures 1.4 and 1.5). Your second literacy cannot use the same websites as your first literacy. You must use four different websites for your two definitions. Copy the definitions and record the URL for the website.

Pick the definition for each literacy that you like best, and record your thoughts on why it is the better definition. Finally, describe which literacy of the two you picked is the one you think is the most important and why.

Literacy 1:	ICT Literacy
Definition 1: ICT literacy can be defined as the skills and abilities that will enable the use of computers and related information technologies to meet personal, educational, and labour market goals.	
URL:	https://www.ets.org/Media/Tests/ETS_Literacy/ICTL_FRAMEWORK.pdf
Definition 2: Literacy with Information and Communication Technology (LwICT) means thinking critically and creatively, about information and about communication, as citizens of the global community, while using ICT responsibly and ethically.	
URL:	http://www.edu.gov.mb.ca/k12/tech/lict/overview/index.html
Best definition and why: The first definition is by far the best. It is more specific and really defines what ICT literacy is all about. The second definition is sound a little like information literacy.	
Literacy 2:	Ecological Literacy
Definition 1: Ecological literacy (also referred to as ecoliteracy) is the ability to understand the natural systems that make life on earth possible. To be ecoliterate means understanding the principles of organization of ecological communities (i.e., ecosystems) and using those principles for creating sustainable human communities.	
URL:	https://en.wikipedia.org/wiki/Ecological_literacy

Figure 1.4: Literacy Worksheet Example

Definition 2:	
Ecological literacy, or eco-literacy, is a term first used in the 1990s by American educator David W. Orr and physicist Fritjof Capra to introduce into educational practice the value and well-being of the earth and its ecosystems. It is a way of thinking about the world in terms of its interdependent natural and human systems, including a consideration of the consequences of human actions and interactions within the natural context.	
URL:	http://www.edu.gov.mb.ca/k12/cur/socstud/global_issues/ecological_literacy.pdf

Best definition and why:
I like the second definition best, again. Not only is it more specific, but it mentions that it includes thinking about how all the systems are interdependent. That makes more sense.

Most important literacy and why:
Of the two literacies I picked, I think that ecological literacy is the most important. It involves knowing what's best for the planet and all life on it. A lack of ecological literacy has led to the many problems we face, today.

Figure 1.4: (*Continued*)

Literacy 1:	
Definition 1:	
URL:	
Definition 2:	
URL:	
Best definition and why:	
Literacy 2:	
Definition 1:	
URL:	
Definition 2:	
URL:	
Best definition and why:	
Most important literacy and why:	

Figure 1.5: Literacy Worksheet

CHAPTER 2

The Information Need and Types of Information

In This Chapter

You will learn:

- What an information need is
- How to write a research question and how to refine it
- Formats, categories, and types of information available to answer your research question

The Information Need

An information need is a question that needs to be answered. That question can take many forms. It can be as simple as what the name of that actress who plays that character on that show, to I have to write a report on some aspect of World War II, where do I begin, to my company is developing a new product, how will consumers feel about our product? In the context of school, this is the research question that you need to answer in your paper or project. It is the hypothesis that you will seek to prove or disprove. In your personal life, it could be finding the best cell phone deal for your intended use or the cheapest price on the best ten-year-old used car. For your professional life, it could be finding how much money the average consumer spends on premium chocolates, which are the top brands, and whether the market is big enough for another competitor.

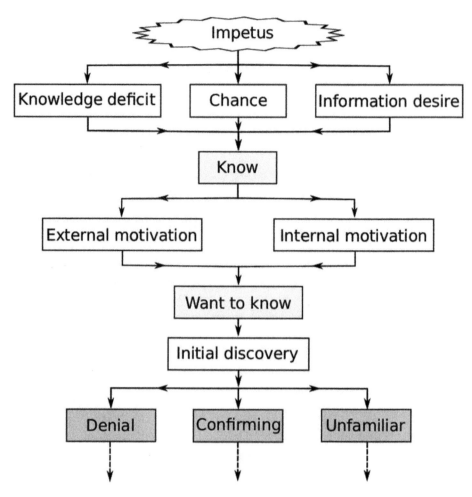

Figure 2.1: Pathways Information Seeking Model—Part 1

Figure 2.1 outlines this process.

The impetus is the force that drives the information seeking process. It can be anything from the need to prepare for a job interview to an unfamiliar word.

Next comes the information need. It may take one of three forms. The knowledge deficit is a need to know. This information need has to be answered, or it will negatively impact events that follow. The opposite of the knowledge deficit is the information desire which is driven by curiosity and is an optional need. This can be a complex or simple need. You don't have to know the answer, but you want to know it. Then there is chance which is when you stumble upon information and want to confirm it, or know more about it.

The information need activates your background knowledge. This is what you already know on the topic. It may be nothing, or it may be very much. If you already know something about the topic, then you can contextualize the information, and have a better idea of where to find the information you need. If you do not know much about the topic, then you are starting with a disadvantage, and may need to find background information to help you contextualize your search.

Now comes your motivation. To have an external motivation is to have the information need placed upon you. Your instructor gave you an assignment, and now you need to find the information to answer that assignment. An internal motivation comes from within you. It is when you want to find the information for personal reasons which may be wanting to know a fact or to develop a greater knowledge of a topic that interests you.

This leads directly to what you want to know. This is the specific question you want to be answered. At this step, you determine the amount, level, and types of information that are needed. Asking the right question is not as easy as it may seem. If your question is a little off, the answer you find will be, too. It may take a few attempts to get the question right. This is normal. Research is an iterative process where you may need to repeat any or a number of the steps to get to the answer you need.

The initial discovery step represents the first of the search steps and the first pieces of information that you find. In the case of simple inquiry, it may be all that is needed. You can find the answer to who played that part in the show very quickly, and count on the answer to be accurate if you know where to look. For a larger or more complex information need, the initial discovery tells you something about the topic you are researching and represents the beginning of the search process.

This leads to the next steps. This is where we have to do something with the information. In denial, you disbelieve the information you found for one reason or another, like the source is not accurate. You could be right, the source of the information may be wrong, and we will talk about how to determine whether an information source is reliable in future chapters. Or you may think that since none of my friends believe that, then it cannot be true. In this case, you are using a social context to give value to information, and ignoring whether the information is correct or not. In any case, denial causes cognitive dissonance, the way we rationalize our inconsistent beliefs (Darity 2008, 601), and that may end the information seeking process.

Another possibility is that the information you first find will be confirming. Confirming information is information that we know how to handle. You received the answer you expected to receive, and/or the information you received fits with what you already know. According to the famed psychologist Jean Piaget, we assimilate information that fits into an existing schema. The hard part is when the information you find does not fit within your knowledge base, and you accommodate unfamiliar information by creating a new schema, a new understanding, a new context for the information in your knowledge base (Elkind 2002, 1897; Goldhaber 2002, 416). There is more to the Pathways Information Seeking Model, and we will get to it in another chapter.

Formulating and Reformulating the Research Question

Now that you have established your information need, you need to formulate a research question that will get you the answer you need. Your question is the starting point for your interaction within the information environment. The question should help you define your information need. It may reflect how much information you want, what categories, formats, and types of information you want.

For example, you start with a simple information need. Your question is succinctly stated, "What is the magnitude of the largest earthquake ever recorded?" This question requires a fact, and can be easily answered with a web search, or in a few more seconds from a print source if you know which ones to grab. You do not need subject knowledge to find this because the context is not geologic information, but facts. You do not need any real knowledge of information systems, either, because a Bing or Google search for "largest earthquake ever recorded" finds your answer. You learn that the largest recorded earthquake took place in Southern Chile near Valdivia on May 22, 1960, and registered a 9.5 on the Moment Magnitude scale ("1960 Valdivia Earthquake" 2016). This is not a research question. Even if you ask what the ten largest earthquakes were, or where do the most earthquakes occur, these are not research questions. Research questions do not look for a fact or a list of facts.

This answer brings up another question, "What is the moment magnitude scale, and how does it compare to the Richter scale?" The first part of this question requires a definition for an answer. Definitions, like facts, are easy to find and do not require a specific information context. However, finding a definition of the moment magnitude scale from a geologic information may give you a better, more detailed definition that may better answer your information need. The first part of this question is also not a research question. There is a definitive answer to this question, and it is easy to find in background information sources.

The second half of this question requires more specific and more in-depth information. You will most likely find the answer in a source like an encyclopedia, and find a better, longer, and more detailed answer in a geology encyclopedia. Using a better resource will require you to gain knowledge of evaluating information and geologic information. This half of the question is not a research question, either. It can be answered from a single source like a subject-specific encyclopedia.

These questions and their answers have led you to another question, "How has earthquake prediction developed, and how good is it today?" This question has more complexity and requires more information than any of the previously asked questions. You may need to find books and articles from the geologic literature, and piece your answer together from these sources because there may not be a definitive answer. This is a research question (Figure 2.2).

A research question takes a deep look at a topic and may require you to conduct original research to find an answer. Research questions should be big in the sense that they ask "why" and "what is the relationship between," as opposed to "when" and "how many." The following is an example of a good research question: "What is the relationship between sleep and a student's academic performance?" This question is not looking for a simple fact, and there may be differing conclusions based on different research studies. You will need to find information from more than one type of information source, and more than one journal article to make sure you have enough information to accurately reflect your topic and answer your question.

If we were to restate the question: "Does the amount of sleep students get reflect in their academic performance?" We could simply answer, "Yes." If we reworded the question to be: "How does the amount of sleep students get impact their academic performance?" We could answer that question by saying, "It has a negative impact." If we tried

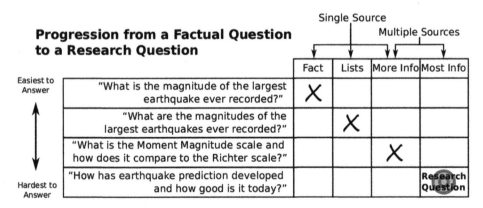

Progression from a Factual Question to a Research Question	Fact	Lists	More Info	Most Info
"What is the magnitude of the largest earthquake ever recorded?"	X			
"What are the magnitudes of the largest earthquakes ever recorded?"		X		
"What is the Moment Magnitude scale and how does it compare to the Richter scale?"			X	
"How has earthquake prediction developed and how good is it today?"				Research Question

Single Source — Multiple Sources

Easiest to Answer ↑ ↓ Hardest to Answer

Figure 2.2: Progression from a Factual Question to a Research Question

re-wording the question, again, this time asking: "How much sleep does a student need to perform well in school?" We could answer that with "12 hours a night." The wording of your question is very important. If you can think of an answer to your question in our head, then it may not be a good research question. Having a good question will improve the whole information seeking process. Do not be afraid to change your question to improve your outcomes.

You need to pay attention to the amount of information your research question leads you to find. This will help you focus your research, and rewrite your question if necessary. The scope of a research question is its breadth or area covered by the question. If our current question finds too much information, we can limit its scope by changing "student" to "high school student" or "college student." The depth of a research question is how much detail is needed to answer your question. This is not specifically addressed in our research question. However, we do not want research from 20 years ago. That information may not include the impacts that current technology has on both sleep and academic behavior. We are going to limit the depth by not using old information. The depth of the information you need will also be determined by the extent of the project you are working on. A research project resulting in a hundred-page report will require much more depth than a five-page summary of sleep and academic performance.

As you begin to explore your topic, you may want or need to modify your research question based on the amount and type of information you find. If you are finding too much information, you may need to narrow your focus and look at a specific aspect of your original thesis. If there is too little information, then you will need to broaden your topic. Remember that research is an iterative process. You may need to adjust your question a few times by reflecting on what you tried, thinking about what might work better, and giving it another try. At this point in the process, you are exploring your options and your interest. Revising your question and re-running a search takes very little time.

There are no hard-and-fast rules that describe too much or too little information, but it is safe to say that if you found so many items that you do not know where to begin or so few that you do not have enough to even start, then you may need to reexamine your question. If your question asks, "What are the environmental causes of cancer in my hometown, and how can they be minimized?" Your search will more than likely return no information. You can broaden the geographic range of your question to the United States, and find some articles. In short, experiment and play with your search. We will talk more specifically about narrowing and broadening your search, evaluating your research process, and evaluating the information you found later on in this book. First, we will examine where to look.

Knowing Where to Look and Publishing Literacy

Information is organized into three broad categories: humanities, social sciences, and sciences. According to the *Merriam-Webster* dictionary, the humanities are "the branches of learning . . . that investigate human constructs and concerns as opposed to natural processes . . . and social relations" (2015). This definition does triple duty. It mentions the sciences as "natural processes" and the social sciences as "social relations." The humanities include philosophy, language, literature, art, and theater. The social sciences include anthropology, psychology, sociology, and business, while the sciences include chemistry, physics, biology, astronomy, and geology.

Using your research question on earthquake prediction from above, you can see that it falls into the sciences. You would not want to use an anthropology encyclopedia to try to find some of your answer to your question, but you would use a science encyclopedia. If your question deals with Ancestral Puebloans, then an anthropology encyclopedia would be a good source to start.

Knowing the broad discipline of your topic helps you to know where to look for information, but you need knowledge of publishing in a discipline to help you understand how information gets into those sources and which sources are best for your research question. This is called publishing literacy (Shapiro and Hughes 1996, 4). For example, while journals are important in all disciplines, they are especially important to the sciences. The latest discoveries are documented in the journal literature first. In the humanities, the newest idea might be too big to be expressed in a journal article, so it is published in a book. Within the humanities, in the arts, new ideas and techniques may be expressed as a series of paintings or a dance.

Figure 2.3 illustrates the scholarly publishing process. The first thing to notice is that before the information is published or presented (the rectangular boxes), there is a review process. The peer review process for the publication of scholarly journal articles is one of the most rigorous and important processes in scholarly publishing. A researcher writes an article about her research project, and what was learned from it. She then submits this article to a scholarly journal, a discipline-specific publication that focuses on publishing research articles intended to be read by other researchers. The article undergoes a peer review where a number of other researchers in the field examine her article to determine if the article's content and quality fit the standards of their

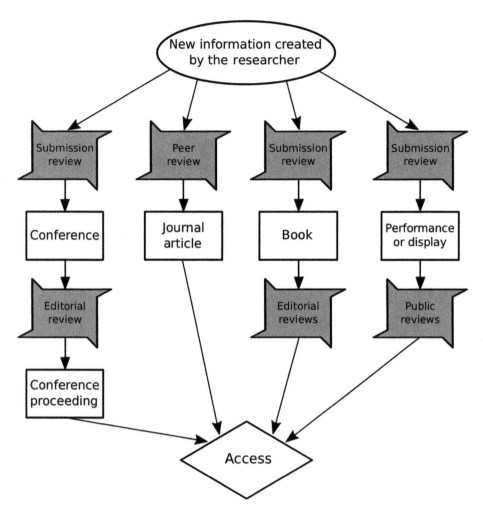

Figure 2.3: The Scholarly Publishing Process

publication. If so, then the article is selected for publication. If the article is not good enough, it is rejected and is not published.

The other publishing and presentation options also have submission reviews. If you have so much material on your topic that you need to write a book, the first thing you would do to get it published is to write a proposal that would include an overview of your book, an outline, your intended audience, possible competitors in the market, and a sample of your writing. Next, an editorial board goes through all the proposals to determine which ones have the most merit. If your proposal is selected, then you receive a contract to write the book, and you are assigned an editor. When you finish the book and submit it, your editor will read it and make sure that the quality is what was expected.

If the manuscript you turn in is not good enough, your book will not be published. If it is, then it enters the publishing pipeline.

Conferences have a submission review that is similar to the others. They also have a second step. To get a conference presentation published in the proceedings, first you have to write out your presentation in the form of an article, then an editor selects the best articles for publication in the conference proceedings, a published record of the best presentation at a conference. If you are in the visual and performing arts, you may be subject to the same kinds of submission reviews for your artwork, dance, and film. In these fields, you may be able to mount an exhibition, a performance, display, or showing, of your work without the initial submission review process. If that is the case, then reviews of the exhibition become very important to evaluate the quality of your work.

Once the publication or presentation of the researchers' ideas has taken place, they have shared their ideas formally with the world, and we can access their research. When we have access to their ideas, we can evaluate them for ourselves, build upon them, and create new knowledge.

There are other publishing processes besides the scholarly publishing model. Magazines, whether published in print or online, are intended for a wide, general audience. They often have an editorial process where reporters pitch ideas, the best are selected and produced. Then these articles may undergo a second editorial review and/or a fact-check before they are published. However, the Internet has introduced an important shortcut to this publishing process that you must be aware of (Figure 2.4).

Submission review, peer review, or editorial review is not necessary to publish anything on the Internet. Anyone can publish anything. Quality is not a concern. Truthfulness is not a concern, and neither are facts. Evaluation of all information is an important process, but it is particularly important when it comes to information found on the Internet. We will discuss this in more detail in another chapter in the book.

Figure 2.4: Filtered versus Unfiltered Access

Formats of Information

Information comes in different formats. It can be in a physical format or a digital format. The format of the information is the least important thing about the information.

Physical

Print is the most common physical, tangible format for recording information that does not require the use of a digital device, but may require the use of an analog device, to "read," decode, or extract the information. We read a book, look at a photograph, or flip through a magazine. Information has been coming in print formats ever since humans learned how to draw on cave walls. Print sources take up a lot of space. They cost more to publish because of the resources consumed to create the object. They cost more to distribute because of their size and weight. The printing and distribution process all add time to the publication of print information. The advent of digital formats for information has made print formats less popular, but many people still prefer the feel of a book in their hands and reading from a print source to using a tablet or reading from a computer screen.

Digital

Digital information is stored as binary code, a series of 1s and 0s. Digital information sources include DVDs, MP3s, databases, websites, and cloud services. We need some kind of digital device to decode the binary and re-create the information in a format that we can interpret through visual or auditory processes. Digital information takes up very little physical space. One DVD can hold thousands of books. Tangible versions of digital information like Blu-rays are subject to the same printing and distribution processes as print sources. However, the Internet allows for instantaneous publication and distribution of digital information. A print publisher needs to estimate the demand for his book. If he overestimates it, he is stuck with expensive stock. If he underestimates the demand for his book, then he incurs additional expenses when he has to print more copies. A digital version of the book can be accessed by one person or one million people and meet any level of demand without taking up any more space or consuming any more resources.

Digital information sources are easier to use, copy, and share, and are more quickly accessible than their print counterparts. However, not everyone has the same access to this information, because Internet access is provided by commercial vendors, and not everyone can afford it. Additionally, certain digital information sources like databases and journals sell their information, and will not let you access it. Libraries buy this information and provide access to it, but this information is expensive. Libraries must pick and choose which information sources they can afford, and that will serve their users the best.

Categories of Information

Information comes in many varieties. In this section, we will look at six broad categories of information that form three dialectic pairs. All information falls into these categories, and often only one category from each pair. For example, a scholarly article written by the researcher who did the project about new astronomical discoveries would be a primary, scholarly, current information. A documentary broadcast on television about Henry IV would be secondary, popular, historical information, and your tweet about how boring the documentary is would be primary, popular current information.

Primary vs. Secondary Information

Primary means direct or firsthand, first in importance, order, and time (Merriam-Webster, Inc. 2016b). *Primary information* is, therefore, firsthand information. It can mean a firsthand account of an event or the results of a research project that is published by the researcher. Secondary information is, therefore, information that is reported secondhand. For example, when a reporter brings you a story about a man who ran into a burning building to save the family dog, it is a secondhand report. When that reporter asks the man who saved the dog what it was like, that person's answer is a firsthand or primary account of the event. Diaries and letters are primary sources of information from the person who wrote them. An autobiography is a primary document because it was written by the person in question. A biography is a secondary information source about the person because it was written by somebody else, and uses many sources of information.

A research article is a good example of a primary information source. It is written by the persons who conducted the research project. A secondary information source would be a source that talks about, uses, or summarizes the research done by others. An article about earthquake prediction written by the persons who conducted the research is a primary source. A book that pulls together many primary and secondary sources of information to present an overview of earthquake predictions is presenting information secondhand making it a secondary source.

Scholarly vs. Popular Information

Scholarly information is a research article. It is information that is cited and verified. It uses primary or new thinking about secondary information sources. It is information intended for an academic or specialized audience. It is information that has been peer-reviewed and published in a scholarly journal.

Popular information is information intended for a broad, general audience that does not take specific background knowledge to understand. It may contain facts that have been verified, and it may have been approved for publication by an editor, but it may have been published, posted, directly to the Internet without any editorial processes, much less a rigorous process like a peer review. For example, an article in *Time* magazine will contain facts that should have been checked. It will be edited and approved for publication, but it is an article that reports on a current event like a protest or rigged pollution testing, and it does not require knowledge of sociology or engineering to understand. Popular information sources are magazines like *Time*, *Vogue*, *National Geographic*, and *Motor Trend*, news sources in print, broadcast or on the web, and many websites. They often feature pictures and videos, whereas scholarly information sources are more likely to have tables and graphs. Scholarly information sources like journals tend to be thicker, and dull-looking compared to their popular counterparts, and they often have the table of contents on the cover. Articles are longer and have citations to scholarly information sources.

Current vs. Historical Information Sources

Current and historical are the last two categories of information. Current information is easy to understand and define. It means new, up to date, or the current conditions or thinking. What constitutes current information varies by discipline. There are exciting astrophysical discoveries made all the time. Current information in astrophysics needs to have been created very recently to reflect the most up-to-date thinking in the field. In contrast, fields like psychology and sociology move a little slower and English literature even more slowly. An article about habitable planets from three years ago is out of date. You would need to find something published more recently if you need that kind of information to answer your research question. However, an article about human behavior that is three years old may have some of the most up-to-date thinking. By contrast, an article about Shakespeare that is 20 years old may reflect the best modern thought on the Bard.

Because current information varies by field, current information sources also vary. Scholarly journals and popular magazines, along with news sources, are all good current information sources. A book may also be a good current information source if the field has not changed since its publication.

Historical information does not mean old information. It means information about the past, as opposed to the current state of affairs. That information could have been gathered, analyzed, and published yesterday. It is the focus on the history and development of ideas or events that make this historical information. New information and new interpretations of past event can be discovered or developed in the present. A historical information source can be any sources of information from an old photograph to a current magazine article. It can be associated with any one of the categories of information in both of the other dialectic pairs.

Knowing which categories of information you will need, and how much information you need from each category, will help you with your research. You may want some popular and historical information to help you better understand your topic and to use in the introduction of your research project, while the bulk of your research will consist of information you gathered from primary, scholarly, current sources.

Types of Information

Finally, information comes in different types and is packaged into sources that reflect these different types. These types of information affect how much and what categories of information you will find in each source. We talked about scope and depth earlier in this chapter, and now we need to add more to the conversation. An information source with a broad scope covers a very broad topic or lots of topics, and one with a narrow scope may cover only one specific aspect of a topic. An information source that lacks depth gives only a little information on a topic, while a source with great depth gives a lot of information. A dictionary has a very wide scope. It collects all or the most commonly used words in a language or field of study. A dictionary has little depth. It entries are brief and to the point.

Background Information Sources

Background information sources, or reference sources as they are called in a library, are designed to bring you quick facts or provide a short overview of a topic. These sources can be very helpful in your research. They provide you with a basic understanding of a topic with which you are unfamiliar and help you focus your research question. They introduce you to the terminology of the field which makes your further searching more efficient and effective. For these reasons, background information sources are a great place to begin your research.

You may not use the information you find in them in your project. Your instructor may want you to use this type of information in your project, but they are invaluable in giving you a place of understanding to start from.

Wikipedia and *Encyclopedia Britannica* are examples of general background information sources. Their scope is very broad, the whole realm of knowledge. They contain tens of thousands or even millions of articles, but their depth is usually limited. They often provide a bibliography of other information sources you can find for further reading on the topic. Other background information sources focus on a specific discipline, like the *McGraw-Hill Encyclopedia of Science and Technology* or the *Stanford Encyclopedia of Philosophy*, or very narrowly focused disciplines, like *Cambridge Illustrated Dictionary of Astronomy* or *Encyclopedia of Group Processes & Intergroup Relations*. These reference sources have a narrower scope than general encyclopedias, but they offer more depth.

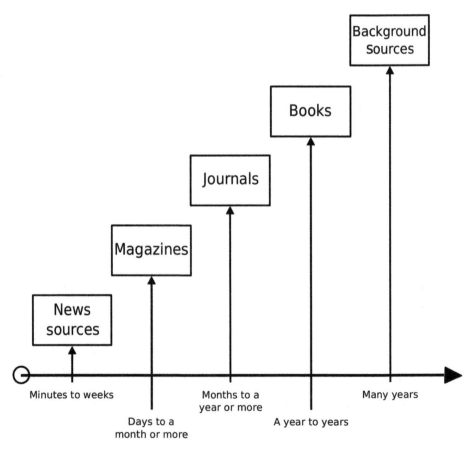

Figure 2.5: Time to Publication for Information Types

Background information sources are always secondary in nature. They can be popular or scholarly. They usually focus on either current or historical information, but may try to do both, which limits their potential depth. There are often many people involved in writing and editing of these sources. The very broad scope of background information sources means that they have the greatest length among the different types of information sources. This length and complexity also mean that it takes a long time to write and compile the information before it can be published, more than any other type of information source. Figure 2.5 illustrates time to publication.

Books

Books have greater depth and narrower scope than background information sources (Figure 2.6). Their length allows them to cover their topic in great detail. Their scope can be broad like the Civil War, or it can be more narrowly focused and cover only General Sherman's March to the Sea.

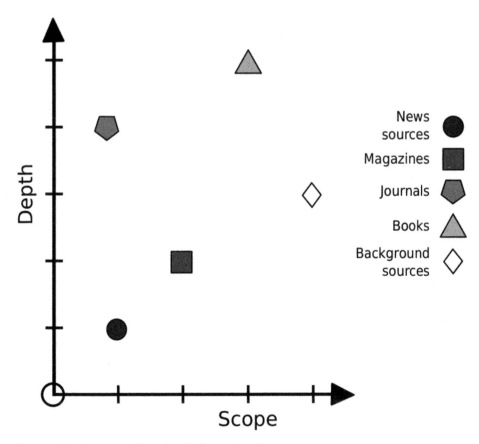

Figure 2.6: Scope and Depth of Information Types

Books will give you more information on your topic than any other type of information. In fact, it may be too much information. You may need to use the table of contents or the index and skim through the book to find the specific information you want to use for your project.

Books can fall into any category of information. They can be primary or secondary, historical or current, popular or scholarly information sources. Books take the second-longest time to reach publication due to their depth and scope.

News Sources

There are many places to get news, the Internet, television, radio, newspapers, and news magazines. An item in a news source will tend to be narrow in scope, as it focuses on one event. The depth also tends to be shallow, as it is more important to publish the information about the event while it is still current. While we are concerned with individual items, it is important to note that news sources taken as a whole have a wide scope due to their broad coverage of events. The intended audience is a broad, popular one. Articles and reports are usually short and secondary in nature. News sources will help you find current information about the latest discoveries for your topic of research, but it will usually not be enough information, and you may need to find the primary information that their report was based on.

News sources have the shortest time to publication. It can be instantaneous. You can be watching events as they happen on the Internet and on television. Television newscasts report on the events of the day. Newspapers report on what happened the day before, and both may follow developing stories.

Magazines

Magazines are designed for a popular audience. Even though it seems like there are at least two magazines for every possible interest, it does not take a subject degree to understand them. This is a very important distinction from their counterparts, journals. Magazines can be print or digital. You can buy print magazines in just about any store. They may have a broad scope like *Time*, or they can be more focused like *Rolling Stone* or *Outside*. They usually have more length than a news source, which allows them to cover a topic with more depth. They can feature interviews with important figures within their scope like a musician or a fashion designer, products reviews, news while providing primary information as when an author describes her experiences hiking in Canyonlands National Park. They do not have scholarly articles, so there is no primary research, but secondary reporting. They can have articles on current or historical topics. Their broad coverage and modest depth may be another good starting point for your research project, and their relatively short time to publication means you can get up-to-date information about events and discoveries. However, their popular nature may preclude their use in a research project.

Journals

Journals publish scholarly articles that have been peer-reviewed. Scholarly articles are written by experts and are intended for students and other experts in that field of study. They detail their experiments and cite the sources they used in their research. Journals have a narrow scope, a specific field, or subfield of study, and they often have great depth because articles can be long and very narrowly focused.

Like their magazine counterparts, there are thousands of journals. However, you cannot buy them in stores or at newsstands, and most of us do not have the $4,400 it costs to subscribe to *International Journal of Radiation Oncology/Biology/Physics* (Elsevier B.V. 2016b), or the nearly $15,000 for a subscription to *Brain Research* (Elsevier B.V. 2016a), nor the interest in reading them. These are institutional subscription prices. This is what it costs your library to subscribe to one of these journals. An individual subscription costs much less, but $809 for *International Journal of Radiation Oncology/Biology/Physics* is still considerably more than a subscription to *Rolling Stone*, and you would think hard about purchasing it which is what libraries have to do.

You may find a number of journal articles that have a similar hypothesis to your research question. These articles may serve to support or disprove what you were thinking at the start of your project. So you may need to adjust your questions and your thinking because articles are great sources of information for your project. A journal article may be too narrowly focused and too detailed for your project. However, you might find some useful information within that article that you will need to extract. Journal articles will help you think about your question, and as they help to support or disprove it, they will help you develop your own thoughts and come to your own unique conclusions about your topic.

Besides publishing primary research, journals publish editorials, news items, and reviews. When using a journal to find a scholarly, primary source, be sure you are not using these items from the journal. It takes time to produce a research article, gathering information, running an experiment, analyzing the results, and writing the report. The publication process takes more time than a magazine article because of the peer review process.

Now that you have knowledge of information sources and publishing, we will move on to finding information in the next chapter.

Vocabulary

background sources

books

current information

depth

digital

historical information

information access

information need

information process

journals

magazines

news sources

popular information

primary information

print

publishing literacy

research question

scholarly information

scope

secondary information

time to publication

Questions for Reflection

What is an information need?

How do you refine your research question?

What are the three broad categories of information?

What is the information seeking process?

What are the differences between primary and secondary information?

What is "time to publication," and how does it impact the information you find?

Would a physical object like a Ming dynasty vase fit into the definition of print?

Assignment

Open your research journal. Select a topic that interests you, and write a research question (Figures 2.7 and 2.8). Record your thoughts on why you believe this is a good research question. Now think about the categories and types of information that you think will best answer your question. Write down your selections and why.

Go to your favorite web search engine, and try searching for your research question or topic. When you have a search that you think worked well enough, write down how many items it retrieved. What categories and types of information are listed on the first page of your results? Will these categories and types of information help you answer your research question? Explain why you think they will or will not work for you. How do the categories and types of information that you wanted to find compare to what you found?

Research question:	What specific effects do a lack of access to the Internet have on students' academic performance?

What makes this a good research questions?
This question cannot be answered with a "yes" or "no," nor can it be answered from a single source of information. You could say the answer it has a negative effect, but I'm not sure that's clear cut, and I'm looking for specific effects.

What categories of information will help you answer this question? Why?
I think primary information will help me the most. I think research articles will answer this question best.
I need current information sources, because the Internet hasn't been around that long.
I think scholarly information will help me the most, but something popular may give me some background information.

What types of information will help you answer this question? Why?
Journal articles will help me the most. That's where the primary research will be.
A background information source or a magazine may give me a foundation about my topic.

Google/Bing search results:	2,380,000 results from Bing

Categories of information retrieved:
I found mostly primary and scholarly types of information. Only one was popular. All were current, because they were published in the last ten years, which will work for my topic.

Will these categories of information help answer your research question? Why or why not?
Yes, the primary articles are scholarly research articles and should help. The secondary articles pull together information from a number of scholarly sources. They have bibliographies.

Types of information retried:
I found journals articles, one magazine article, and one web page.

Will these types of information help answer your research question? Why or why not?
The journal articles should help. The magazine article and web page were too broad in scope, and not on my topic.

Figure 2.7: Research Question Worksheet Example

How do the categories and types of information that you wanted to find compare to what you found?
I was surprised I found as many primary and scholarly information sites as I did. I thought there would be a lot more popular information.
I also thought I would find a lot of personal websites, but I found a lot of journals articles.
I think I found good information to use in my research.

Figure 2.7: (Continued)

Research question:	
What makes this a good research questions?	
What categories of information will help you answer this question? Why?	
What types of information will help you answer this question? Why?	
Google/Bing search results:	
Categories of information retrieved:	
Will these categories of information help answer your research question? Why or why not?	
Types of information retried:	
Will these types of information help answer your research question? Why or why not?	
How do the categories and types of information that you wanted to find compare to what you found?	

Figure 2.8: Research Question Worksheet

Librarians and Library Services

In This Chapter

You will learn:

- Why you should not have library anxiety
- What librarians do
- How they can help you with your research project
- What services are offered that will help with your research project

Library Anxiety

When you say the word "library," people think of an old brick public library downtown, the big building on the campus of the university, or the room in a school packed with books and computers. Library is a place, a physical space, that can be visited or avoided. With so many materials and databases available online, this is not such a true statement. In any event, those who avoid libraries may suffer from library anxiety. Library anxiety is a fear of the library or the librarian. This fear stems from the intimidating size of the library, the confusing organization of materials, not knowing where or how to start using the library, the old person sitting behind the desk and watching you.

A research article by Blundell and Lambert cites a number of other research projects that showed library anxiety leads to poor academic performance (2014, 236). Project Information Literacy has been studying students' information literacy behavior since 2008 (Project Information Literacy 2016a). In a summary of their years of research, they stated that 80% of students have tremendous problems starting a research assignment while at the same time tremendously ignoring the help librarians will provide (Head 2013, 474–75). Project Information Literacy also reported some of the adjectives that come to mind when students think about doing a research project. They included angst, confused, dread, fear, overwhelmed, and stressed (Head and Eisenberg 2009). In a qualitative study of library anxiety, one student was quoted as saying that being in the library was like being in a foreign country and not knowing the language (Mellon 2015, 279). She does not understand the library environment nor how to operate in this context.

Mellon's research also found something more troubling. She discovered that students feel inadequate and embarrassed by their lack of knowledge about the library. Compounding the problem is the belief that their friends and classmates are not having the same problems (Mellon 2015, 279). This is a particularly destructive belief. It will prevent you from getting the help you need and deserve. It is easy to tell some not to be worried. That things will be fine. That everyone is in the same boat as you are. However, that does not solve the problem.

The Librarian

Perhaps knowing what librarians do will help. Libraries are not just places to access databases and check out a book. They are places that specialize in providing students with research assistance. In other words, they exist to help you find the information you need, and librarians are the people who provide that assistance. Librarians have unique jobs. One of the most important aspects of their job is to provide research help. Librarians are professional question answerers. They get paid to answer *your* questions in a courteous and professional manner. This means that they give every person their respect, their full attention, and all the assistance they can offer without judgment. They are your tour guide in the foreign country that is the library, and they speak the language fluently.

Librarians will be found at a desk that may be called a reference desk, help desk, or question desk. The terminology is changing and can be confusing. "Reference" is an old term that many libraries still use, but it no longer conveys what librarians can do to help you. No matter what the desk is called, the librarian will help you with your questions about the library and all of its information sources and services. No one expects you to remember everything you have learned reading this book. Fortunately, there is someone who already knows it all and can help you with it, your librarian.

You may feel intimidated or a little embarrassed to approach the librarian. They might look busy, frazzled, old, confused, or mean. They may appear to be watching you closely, but what they are really trying to do is establish eye contact and say "hello." It is normal to have reservations. However, the more you know about libraries and the role of librarians, the less anxiety you will have (Gross and Latham 2007), and one of the best ways to learn what your library can do to help you is to ask the librarian. So if you are nervous, take a deep breath and approach the librarian.

Research Help

Librarians will be able to help you with many aspects of your research. They can help you pick a database to search. They can help you find good search terms. They can help you formulate your search statement, and they can show you what special features a database has and how to use them, like getting citations for the items on your marked list. They can help you search the catalog or find books on the shelf and help you find a background source. They can help you find out what journals the library has available in full text and in print.

Interlibrary Loan

If you find an article that is not available in full text either in your library's print collection or databases, or if you know of a book you need that your library does not own, then you should use interlibrary loan (ILL). This is an important service that libraries offer. ILL is a formal method for sharing materials between libraries that give libraries access to more materials than they can afford to buy. An item you need will be obtained by your library from another library. If it is a book, then there will be a checkout period for its use. If it is an article, you will receive a photocopy or an electronic version of the article that is yours to keep.

To use your library's ILL service, you will need to fill out either a print or an electronic form. ILL is often free for materials that are located within an affiliated group of libraries called a consortium. Charges may apply to materials that come from outside this group or beyond a geographical area, such as the state you are in. When there is a charge that you have to pay, you must decide how valuable this information is to you and what you are willing to pay for it. Charges are implemented to cover costs of offering the services and shipping materials.

Materials that need to be shipped will take one to two weeks to arrive. This is why it is important to start your research early. If you need a book your library does not have and you waited to start your research, it may not arrive in time for you to use it in your research project. How fast an item arrives depends on a number of factors, and these factors are beyond the control of your local library. Articles, on the other hand, are commonly transmitted electronically from the lending library, the library that has the material, to the borrowing library, the library where you are located. Using this method, an electronic copy of an article may arrive in one or two days.

Library Instruction

Besides the personalized help you can get from a librarian at the reference desk, librarians also teach groups of students how to use library resources. This is called library instruction or information literacy instruction. Your instructor may arrange to take your class to the library or have the librarian come to your class, and show you some databases and search techniques tailored to the needs of your class. Library instruction is a good introduction to finding the information you need. The drawback is that often librarians have only one class period to provide this instruction. That means the instruction will have a broad scope with only one or two instructional goals like introducing psychology students to PsycInfo and APA style.

Instruction may raise more questions than it answers. That is a good thing. Research guides may be handed out or referenced in electronic form linked from the library homepage that you can use after class to help you answer some of those questions you may have. You know where to find the librarians, and you know they welcome your questions. In fact after an instruction session, librarians are happy to see the students they taught, because it shows an interest in the research process. Raising awareness of library services and generating new questions is part of the purpose of library instruction. Asking a question means you have learned the most important lesson of the instruction session that librarians are there to help you answer your questions.

Librarians are your allies in the research process. They know how to find information and what resources and services the library has that may be of assistance to you. Their job is to help you find this information and use these resources and services efficiently and effectively. Be sure to take advantage of this service and ask your librarian for help.

Vocabulary

borrowing library

consortium

information literacy instruction

interlibrary loan

lending library

librarian

library anxiety

library instruction

reference desk

Questions for Reflection

What is library anxiety, and how can it be overcome?

What kinds of help can you get from a librarian?

How can interlibrary loan help you with your research?

What is the purpose of library instruction?

Assignment

Open your research journal and write three questions related to your research that you would ask a librarian (Figures 3.1 and 3.2).

Next, reflect on what you learned from this book about information literacy.

Questions for the librarian about research project	
1.	What database is best to use for finding information on how hydraulic fracturing is causing earthquakes and what the consequences of this might be?
2.	Where would I find background sources on both earthquakes and hydraulic fracturing?
3.	My professor remembers an article from this year about fracking that had a color illustration of it. Is there some way I can find this?
Reflection on information literacy	
What was learned:	I learned how to use Boolean operators AND, OR, and NOT. I learned about citation styles. I did not know there were some many and that there are many places to help getting them right.

Figure 3.1: Questions and Information Literacy Worksheet Example

	I also learned why it is important to evaluate sources of information and how to do it. I feel better about finding good information now. I learned how to use facets to limit my search to full-text journal articles which is a big help when it comes to finding scholarly information right now.
Most important knowledge gained and why:	I didn't know how to construct a good search. Learning about Boolean operators has changed the way I search databases. My searching is much better and I am finding better quality information that relates to my topic.

Figure 3.1: (*Continued*)

Questions for the librarian about research project	
1.	
2.	
3.	
Reflection on information literacy	
What was learned:	
Most important knowledge gained and why:	

Figure 3.2: Questions and Information Literacy Worksheet

CHAPTER 4

Finding Information

In This Chapter

You will learn:

- What a database is
- How to search a database to find resources
- How search works
- How to select search terms

Indexes

Indexes are finding aids. They make it easier to find information. This book has an index that helps you find specific pieces of information within it. In the print era before computers, bibliographies, a list of information resources related by topic, focused on helping researchers find books with the information they needed. As publishing developed and magazines, journals, and newspapers were published, indexes were developed to help people find information within those publications. These print indexes often indexed the contents of many magazines and journals, and they took up a lot of space in libraries. Finding information sources on your topic in bibliographies and print indexes took a lot of time.

To use a print index or bibliography, you would look for a subject term of interest, the index entry, then listed under that term were all the books, magazine or journal articles on that topic. That information was presented in a bibliographic format, which means it was a citation to the material. You would write the citation information down, then use another print index, the library card catalog, to see if your library had the materials you wanted.

These early print indexes and bibliographies were the print equivalent of our digital databases. Bibliographies are still around, and can be very helpful, but their role in the information context has greatly diminished. Databases allow us to search in seconds what used to take hours to do in a print index, and because of this great increase in efficiency, print indexes have all but disappeared.

What Is a Database?

A database is a collection of records. A record is a collection of fields. A field is a container for specific information. While this definition may not be the most helpful, Figure 4.1 may better explain these relationships.

Databases are made up of thousands or millions of records. A small library may have only a thousand records in its library catalog, the database of all the materials in the library. Google, on the other hand, indexes more than 41 billion web pages (WorldWideWebSize.com 2016). Looking at a record will show you the types of information available in the database. Figure 4.2 illustrates a single record taken from the PubMed database (http://www.ncbi.nlm.nih.gov/pubmed/).

The field names are listed in the left-hand column, and these names tell you the kind of information you will find. The first field in the record is the title of the article, "Cognitive influence of a 5-h ENERGY® shot . . ." Every record in this database has an article title field that specifically and only contains the title of the article. The names of the authors are put in the author field, the abstract goes in the abstract field, and so on. This database does not contain the full text of the article. If it did, there would be another field, a very big one, which contained the whole text of the article. Every record in this database has all of these fields. If an article does not have an author, then the author field is still there, but it is left blank.

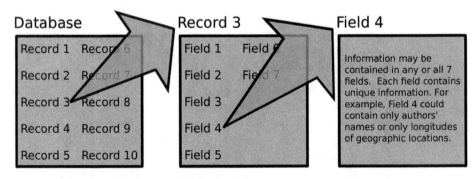

Figure 4.1: Relationship between a Database, a Record, and a Field

Field Names:	Information Contained in the Field:
Article Title:	Cognitive influence of a 5-h ENERGY® shot: Are effects perceived or real?
Authors:	Buckenmeyer PJ[1], Bauer JA[2], Hokanson JF[3], Hendrick JL[4].
Journal Name & Publication Info:	Physiol Behav. 2015 Dec 1;152(Pt A):323-7. doi: 10.1016/j.physbeh.2015.09.003. Epub 2015 Sep 21.
Contact Information:	State University of New York at Cortland, Kinesiology Department, PO Box 2000, Cortland, NY 13045, USA. Electronic address: Phil.Buckenmeyer@cortland.edu.
Abstract:	With the gain in popularity and use of "functional energy drinks" (FEDs), manufacturers of these beverages have been making greater claims as to their benefits on a number of performance factors including mental alertness, energy, and physical performance. Few experimental studies have been conducted on FEDs, and no study to date has examined their effects over time. This study looked at the effects of consumption of a 5-h ENERGY® shot (5-HES) on various cognitive functions across five hours on 24 college-aged students using a double-blind, cross-over, placebo-based design. Participants completed a series of five computer-based tests before ingesting the beverage (either 5-HES or placebo) and then completed the tests for each of the next five hours (morning to midday). One week later, they repeated the process with the other beverage. While 90% of participants subjectively thought that the 5-HES was effective at one-hour post-ingestion, no evidence was found to support an enhanced effect on recognition, reaction time, short-term and working memory, or attention capacity. In conclusion, the 5-h Energy Shot® did not significantly improve short- or long-term cognitive function for selected computer-based tasks despite a high level of perception that it was working effectively compared to a placebo with college-aged participants.
Subject Terms:	Cognitive function; Functional energy drink; Perception
Article ID Number:	PMID: 26394126 [PubMed—in process]

Figure 4.2: Record from PubMed Database

Databases have a very broad scope, and even databases that are narrowly focused try to index the entire contents of many information resources, although their depth varies. Print indexes and bibliographies are shallow. They give you enough information to find the original source, the citation information, and sometimes they give you a short summary, called an abstract, and/or a critical comment about the information source, called an annotation. Databases have these same features; in addition, they often have the full text of the information source, the whole article, which gives them tremendous depth as well. These are called full-text databases. Some databases contain citation and abstract information only, while others databases are a hybrid, containing full-text information for some of their sources and citation/abstract information for other information sources.

Because databases are digital, they are updated regularly. The updating can happen every day, and include material published the previous day. For example, *ProQuest Newspapers,* which is a database of newspapers, updates or publishes new entries for articles within the *Chicago Tribune* just hours after the paper is published! Some databases are updated on a regular schedule like once a month or once a quarter. The schedule depends on the type of information the database includes.

Free Databases

Databases fall into two broad categories: free and fee. Google and Bing are examples of free databases, though we call them search engines. You do not pay to use them to conduct a search or to access the information they provide. These resources try to index the entire visible web. When you do a Google search, you can find information on websites that are available for everyone to access. This is the visible web. The information you find on the visible web can be great, or it can be horrible. As we discussed in the previous chapter, anyone can create and post information to the web. You always need to evaluate your information, but information from the visible web should be examined very closely. We will talk about how to do just that in Chapter 7.

A more scholarly example of a free database is Directory of Open Access Journals (DOAJ, http://www.doaj.org/doaj). It indexes free scholarly journal articles. These kinds of sources are called open access. There are many open access scholarly journals, and a growing number of open access textbooks but small compared to their commercial counterparts. The open access movement is a response to the traditional scholarly publishing model where the articles, peer review, and editorial leadership were all provided free of charge to a publisher because of the nature of the tenure system at colleges and universities that require professors to perform scholarly activities like research, writing articles, writing reviews, peer-reviewing, and editing for a journal. These publishers take advantage of the free materials and labor, and then turn around and sell this information at very high costs back to the libraries of colleges and universities where the information originated.

Governments have taken notice of this issue. The National Institutes of Health began requiring that articles based on research done with one of its grants be added to its database, PubMed, within 12 months of their original publication ("NIH Public Access Policy" 2015). This plan has been expanded to all government agencies with at least $100 million in research and development funds (Stebbins 2013). The European Union is following suit, and by 2020 all research funded with public money must be available through open access ("Guidelines on Open Access to Scientific Publications and Research Data in Horizon 2020" 2016, 4).

Fee Databases

Fee databases or commercial databases charge you to use their resources. Some databases let you search their resources for free, but then charge you to view the information you find. One article can easily cost you $40, and you need to make your decision to purchase the article from looking at the abstract. Others charge you to use the database, but then the information you find is free. Fee databases are part of the invisible web. They cannot be accessed by everyone, and the information they contain may not be found with a web search. This is what makes them invisible on the web.

The information this type of database contains comes from news sources, magazines, journals, books, and reference sources. Beside these print-equivalent formats, databases may also contain images and videos. Most of the resources in fee databases come from commercial sources. The information is collected and organized by commercial database vendors. Both of these groups have a profit motive. They want to make money off the information they have produced and packaged. Publishers charge database vendors to use their materials. Database vendors charge users for aggregating information from many sources and for providing a search mechanism to find the information. For example, you can buy a copy of *People* at the store, or you can read it on Academic Search Premier, which is a database that includes the full text of many magazines and journals put together by the EBSCOhost.

Of course, buying a subscription to *People* is a lot cheaper than buying a subscription to Academic Search Premier. Fortunately, libraries purchase these resources and make them available to you at no cost. While these databases are very expensive, they do cost less than purchasing everything they include separately. The fact that you pay for this information is no guarantee of quality. Information that you find in databases still needs to be evaluated.

Searching Databases

Databases are designed to be searched. To make searching efficient, database have an index where the actual search takes place. Entries in the index point to records in the database. Database searches are done by programs called search engines. Google and Bing are search engines that search their indexes of web pages and find records based on the words you choose to use in your search. It is easy to search a database. Type something in the search box, hit Enter, and you should find some information. Searching a database well takes more skill.

The records your search finds are called search results. Initially, these records are displayed in a shortened form called the results list. When you select an item from the results list to view, you get the full record; all the fields in the record display their full content.

Your search terms are the words you enter into the search box. We call these terms your keywords. Keywords are one word or a few words that describe a topic or subject. When you search a database for "climate change," you are technically using a keyword phrase. This two-word phrase describes a single topic. A database search with this phrase will likely retrieve many records. Your retrieval will be high. There will be a long results list to look at. However, the relevance of the material to your research question could be low. We use the terms "relevance" and "retrieval" in information literacy to help us understand the quality of the search we performed.

Retrieval is simply how many items you find, and relevance is how appropriate those items are for your research. Even though you found many records, they are not all that you want, and you will have to look through many records to find the good items. We would describe this search as having high retrieval and low relevance. If you do a very specific search and find only a few articles, but most of the information is appropriate for your topic, then we would describe your search as having low retrieval and high relevance. Any search with low retrieval may mean that you did not find enough information. That could be from a lack of information on your topic or a bad search that used the wrong keywords to search the database. Low relevance also is an indicator of a bad search based on poor keyword choice, or it could mean that you need to narrow the focus of your research. You want to find a balance between retrieval and relevance. What that balance looks like will differ from person to person.

Some words in databases are not searchable. These words are called stop words. Stop words are usually short and are very common words like "the," "a," "an," "was," and "to." Other stop words are words that have a special meaning to the database and are used in searching, like the Boolean operators, AND, OR, and NOT. You do not need to capitalize the operators when using them in your searches. They are capitalized here for illustrative purposes. You use Boolean operators to tell the search engine specifically how to look for your information. These words are part of the commands you can give to search engines that will help you find exactly what you are looking for. We will examine these commands in the section entitled Advanced Searching, later in the chapter. Knowing how a database is structured and searched will help you find the information you need quickly, but a basic search can be done without this knowledge.

Basic Search

The search screen you see at Google or Bing is an example of a basic search screen. It has a box where you input the keywords you want to search (Figure 4.3).

Unless you know how to enter advanced commands, the search performed when you hit the Enter key will be a basic search, too. The search engine will follow its predefined rules, using its standard algorithm to analyze all the keywords you entered and interpret how to do the search, then search in a predefined selection of fields, finally returning your results. Commercial databases and library catalogs have basic search screens as well. It is a very simple way to conduct a search, but not necessarily the best. It is a quick way to get an idea of how much information is available on your topic, but the basic search is making all the decisions for you about how to find the information you want. A better option is to use an advanced search.

Figure 4.3: Basic Search Box

Advanced Search

The advanced search screens give you control over how your search is carried out (Figure 4.4). You can pick the specific fields you want to search and easily specify how you want to combine your search terms. When you use the advanced search screen, it is easier to understand what the search is doing which also makes it easier to modify your search to change the number of results you receive.

The advanced search screen contains multiple search boxes and drop-down boxes to pick which fields you want to search, and which operators you want to use. However, you still need to know what the commands are to use this search screen effectively.

Search Mechanics

We all use technology like our smart phones, Google, and word processors. But do we take advantage of all of their features? Do we even know what all of the features are? If we knew what the features were and how they worked, would our interactions with technology be better? In the case of database searching, the answer is yes. Search engines are the tools that allow us to search databases. The better we know how to use this tool, the better our search results will be. Search engines use commands to search databases. Using these commands to create and build searches is called search mechanics. These are the mechanisms that make the search work.

When you put together these commands with your keywords, you create a search statement. For example, if you did a search for "inflation," then you have a very simple search statement that does not need any commands. It will use the search engine defaults to execute your search, and retrieve too much information. In this case, it retrieved

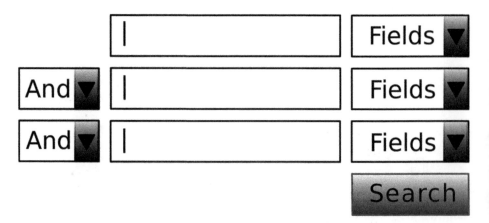

Figure 4.4: Advanced Search Screen

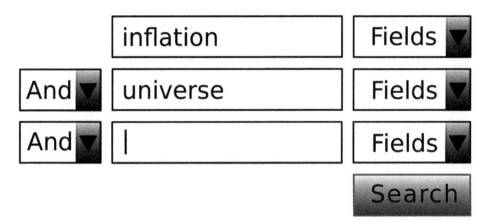

Figure 4.5: Two-Line Advanced Search

more than 37,000 results for Academic Search Premier. Using the advanced search screen and placing inflation in the first box and universe in the second box, we are telling the search engine to use the Boolean operator AND between our keywords.

This search returns 2,700 results (Figure 4.5). Still too much, but a big improvement. We could add an additional keyword to the third line and further limit our retrieval while improving our relevance. We will begin our exploration of search commands by looking at Boolean operators.

Boolean Operators

One very important set of commands are the Boolean operators. Boolean operators were developed by George Boole, an English mathematician in the 19th century (Lerner and Lerner 2013, 27). The operators are:

- AND
- OR
- NOT

Boolean operators are used to control how your keywords are combined and interact with each other in your search statement. Boolean operators are used in the search engines of all commercial databases and in web search engines. The AND operator finds the intersection of two or more keywords. Of all the records in the database, AND finds only the records that contain both or all of your keywords. It narrows your search, retrieving fewer results, but increases the relevance of the results. We use Venn diagrams to illustrate how Boolean operators work. Figure 4.6 is a Venn diagram that illustrates how the

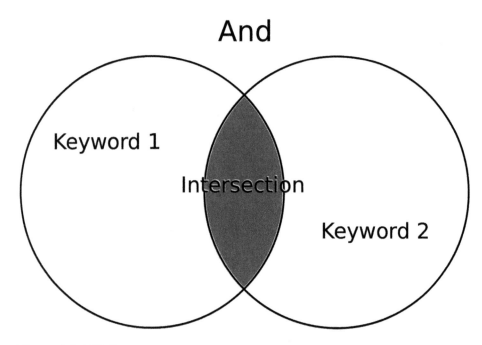

And

Keyword 1

Intersection

Keyword 2

Figure 4.6: AND Operator

AND operator works with two keywords. The gray area in the middle is where our two ideas overlap or intersect. This area represents the records in the database that mention both of our search terms.

If we substitute real keywords for the placeholders Keyword 1 and Keyword 2 we can look specifically at the results of combining keywords with AND. In the previous example, assume we searched for "piracy AND musicians." Let us also assume that there are 5,000 records in our database on piracy, and 20,000 records on musicians. However, there are only 150 records that mention both piracy and musicians. Our search finds only those 150 records. The part where the two circles overlap in the Venn diagram represents those 150 records.

If we want the intersection of three keywords, "piracy," "musicians," and "money," our search statement should look like this:

- piracy AND musicians AND money

The Venn diagram for this search is illustrated in Figure 4.7.

The AND operator is the most important of the three Boolean operators. It earns this status because it brings your ideas, expressed as your keywords, together finding where they intersect. This is exactly what you need to find information that addresses your research question. You can construct excellent searches using only AND.

The Boolean operator OR finds the union of ideas (Figure 4.8). When you join keywords with OR, you find every instance of all of

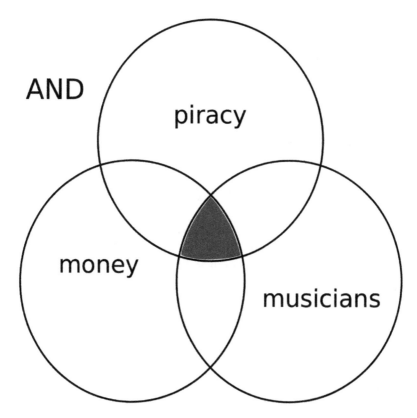

Figure 4.7: AND Search with Three Keywords

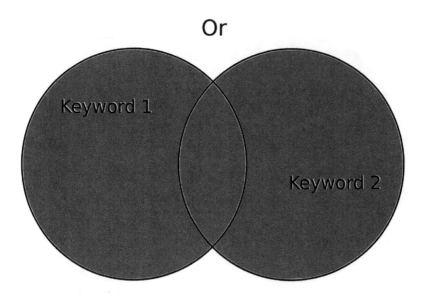

Figure 4.8: OR Operator

those keywords in the database. The OR operator broadens your search, retrieving more results while decreasing relevance.

If we substitute OR for the AND in our previous example, our search is:

- piracy OR musicians

With 5,000 articles about piracy and 20,000 articles about musicians in our database, and an overlap of 150 articles which we learned from our AND search with the same keywords, we can calculate how many records in the database have any or all of our keywords. It is 5,000 + 20,000–150. We subtract the overlap so we do not count records twice. There are 24, 850 records in our database that contain any or all of our keywords.

The OR operator serves a very different purpose than the AND operator. The OR operator should be used to group synonyms together. For example, synonyms for musicians are bands, performers, musical groups, and artists. If you use "artists," you need to realize that its meaning is much broader than "musicians," and you will retrieve many records that contain information about nonmusical artists. You can combine all of these synonyms into a set with the search statement:

- musicians OR bands OR performers OR musical groups OR artists

The section on nesting, later in the chapter, will explain what you do with this and why it is important.

The last Boolean operator is NOT (Figure 4.9). It is very specialized, and there are fewer instances when it would be appropriate to use it.

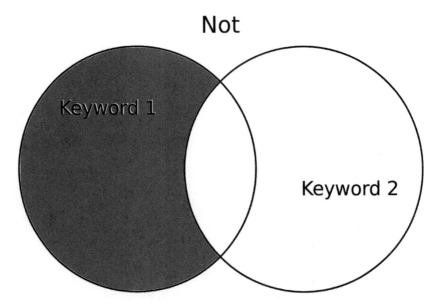

Figure 4.9: NOT Operator

Use the NOT operator to exclude ideas from your search, narrowing your results and increasing relevance.

For example, if you want to find articles on piracy that do not talk about musicians, your search would be:

■ piracy NOT musicians

With 5,000 records about piracy, 20,000 records about musicians, and 150 records that mention both, our search would find 4,850 records that include the keyword piracy, but do not contain the keyword musicians. Clearly, this did not narrow our search very much. There may be a better way to find what we want without using NOT. Experiment with your keywords, and Boolean operators and see what happens. It may help you focus your research question.

The NOT operator is the most difficult of the Boolean operators to use. You may never need to use the NOT operator. It can be useful to exclude ideas that are not the focus of your research or ideas that add ambiguity to your search, although you also run the risk of losing relevant results.

Phrase Searching and Proximity

We mentioned a keyword phrase earlier in this chapter when we talked about climate change. This is a two-word phrase that stands for one concept. If you search for:

■ climate change

search engines will interpret this to mean:

■ climate and change

Most search engines recognize double quotation marks as the phrase operator. To do a search for the keyword phrase, enclose it in quotation marks:

■ "climate change"

This search issues a command to the search engine that tells it that the word "change" must be found adjacent to "climate" and following it for there to be a successful match to a record. This makes a phrase search a highly specialized AND search. A phrase search will lower your retrieval and increase your relevance, dramatically. This effect can be great for your search, giving you the results you want. It can also be a disaster. The narrowing effect may eliminate all records from your search or give you too few to work with. This may happen because the phrase you used is not the right one to describe your topic or there is simply not much information on your topic. In any event, you may need to rethink the keywords and phrases you are using in your search statement or rethink your research question. With that said, it is much better to search for "special interest groups" than to search for *special AND interest AND groups.*

Proximity searching is a less specific form of phrase searching. It allows for more variation in what can be retrieved. Unlike the Boolean operators, proximity operators are not standardized and will be different in different databases. You will need to consult the help screens of the database you are searching to find out what the proximity operators are. We will use N/# and W/# as examples of the two different kinds of proximity operators. N/# means that your keywords need to be within the specified number of words of each other and in no particular order. Here is a sample search statement:

- "carbon dioxide" n/5 tundra

This search statement tells the search engine to find the phrase "carbon dioxide," then find the keyword "tundra," but only return the results if "tundra" is within five words either before or after "carbon dioxide."

W/# has the same meaning with one addition. The words must be in the order specified by the search statement.

- legalization w/2 marijuana

In this example, "legalization" needs to be within two words of "marijuana," but "legalization" must come first.

Proximity searching, like NOT searching, is very specialized and has a smaller application. Consider reconstructing your search to avoid proximity. On the other hand, phrase searching is extremely useful and very powerful.

Nesting

Nesting is used to group synonyms and control the order of execution of your search statement. Search engines have predefined rules about what to do when they come across Boolean, phrase, and proximity operators, and these rules include which ones to evaluate first. The order operators are evaluated in is the order of execution. Typically, AND is executed first, then NOT, and finally OR. Order of execution impacts your search results, and you need to know how this works in order to get the results you want. For example, your research topic is the impact of climate change on whales. You developed a Boolean search statement complete with synonyms that look like this:

- "climate change" or "global warming" and whales or cetaceans

You know exactly what you want the search to retrieve, but based on the predefined order of execution, the search engine sees your search statement very differently than you do. This is what it sees:

- ("global warming" and whales) or "climate change" or cetaceans

In other words, your search is going to find all the records that mention both global warming and whales, then it will add to those results all the records that mention climate change, then add that to all the records that mention cetaceans. That is not what you want. The search you want should look like this:

- ("climate change" or "global warming") and (whales or cetaceans)

The parentheses control the order of execution. They tell the search engine which part of the search needs to be done first. In this case, the search engine would execute the search for "climate change OR global warming" first. It will hold these results as a set, then look for "whales OR cetaceans" and create a set from that information. Finally, it will AND those two sets of information together to achieve the results you want.

Using the advanced search screen in the database you choose for your research, your search should look like Figure 4.10.

To make the best use of this search, place one key concept and its synonyms on one line, using OR to combine them into a set. The advanced search screen automatically places parentheses around the content of each line.

The default is to AND the contents of one line to another. So you do not have to change the Boolean operator. On the second line, place your second key concept and the keywords or phrases that describe it, and use ORs, again, to combine the all the keywords on that line. This search is looking exactly like our good search statement above to the search engine, and will return exactly the same results.

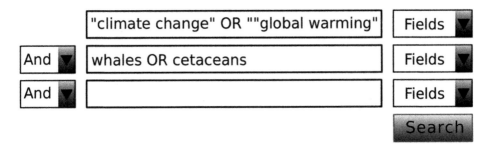

Figure 4.10: Complex Search on an Advanced Search Screen

Stemming

Search engines automatically look for plural or singular forms of the words when they search. If you search for "frog," you will find all instances of "frogs" as well. Just a few years ago, you had to tell search engines to look for plurals by using a truncation symbol. To find all the records with either "frog" or "frogs," you entered this search:

- frog*

The truncation symbol is still available to be used in your searches of commercial databases, but now it is used for word stemming. Stemming is looking for multiple forms of a word based on word endings. If you were interested in everything involving economics, production, and unemployment, you may want to stem "economics" to "econom*." This will find economic, economics, economist, econometrics, economically, and economy, among others. This will increase your retrieval, but may wreak havoc on your relevance. The rest of your search statement will give your search more context and help to eliminate some of the forms of the word you do not want. Use stemming carefully when you think it is necessary, but look closely at the results you retrieve for relevance.

Using Help Screens

Help screens are available in most databases. Often, there is a link to "Help" in the upper-right corner of the page, but you may have to look around to find the link. Help screens provide information on how to search the database, fields, and operators that are available, any special features or searches that you can use, and viewing and saving your results. If you are unsure about a search you are performing, a quick look at the help screens may answer your questions.

Revising the Search

When you search a database, chances are your first search will not be perfect. It will retrieve either too many or too few items. Knowing how a search works allows you to quickly refine your search. In the sample worksheet in Figure 4.11, we have entered a search that found too few items. To use the worksheet, you OR together all the words in one row, then you AND together each of the rows. This worksheet is based on the advanced search screens you will see in a number of databases and represents the way you should use the advanced search screens to construct your search statements.

You can see that our search had four key concepts that were ANDed together. There are no synonyms, and the search is spelled out at the

Search Worksheet

		1st keyword	OR	2nd keyword (synonym)	OR	3rd keyword (synonym)
	1st key concept	dogs				
AND	2nd key concept	"mental health"				
AND	3rd key concept	"elderly patients"				
AND	4th key concept	"nursing homes"				
Search Statement						
dogs AND "mental health" AND "elderly patients" AND "nursing homes"						

Figure 4.11: Search Worksheet with Too Narrowly Focused Search

Search Worksheet

		1st keyword	OR	2nd keyword (synonym)	OR	3rd keyword (synonym)
	1st key concept	dogs	OR	cats	OR	pets
AND	2nd key concept	"~~mental~~ health"				
AND	3rd key concept	"~~elderly~~ patients"				
~~AND~~	~~4th key concept~~	~~"nursing homes"~~				
Search Statement						
(dogs OR cats OR pets) AND health AND patients						

Figure 4.12: Revised Search Worksheet to Increase Retrieval

bottom of the form in the Search Statement section. Unfortunately, this search found no results. We need to broaden this search to retrieve some information.

There are a number of things we can do to broaden this search. First, we can delete one of the key concepts. Three ANDs is a broader search than four ANDs. So we will delete the fourth key concept because that is the least important one to our research question.

Next, we can broaden our keywords. For example, "health" will retrieve more results than the phrase "mental health," and "patients" will retrieve more than "elderly patients." Finally, we can use synonyms to expand the search as well as increase our retrieval. We can add "OR cats OR pets" to the second and third keyword boxes for our first concept. Figure 4.12 shows the revised worksheet.

Notice how our search statement has changed to reflect the new information on the worksheet. We now are using parenthesis to create a set of related keywords for our first key concept. The changes worked. The search statement now retrieves many records. In fact, it is retrieving too many records. We have made our search too broad.

We need to narrow the focus of our search statement, readjust our research question, and find some keywords that will give us fewer and better records, but not zero records like our first attempt. The problem with our search lies either in the keywords we are using or in our research topic. The fastest and easiest way to narrow your search and retrieve fewer records is to add a line to your search. "Nursing homes" was a key concept in our first failed search, but with the synonyms and broader concepts, it might work this time. To help it out, we will also add a synonym to that line. "Patients" might have been a bad choice for a keyword. We are really interested in "elderly patients," but that did not work. So this time, we will try "elderly," relying on the "nursing homes" concept to give context to "elderly." We really wanted information on "mental health," too. We changed that to "health" to broaden our search. Now that we have too much information, we will change that back to "mental health." This is our new search.

Good news! This search seems to work! We retrieved a manageable number of records (Figure 4.13). The search better reflects our interest and our original research question. Remember, the research process is iterative. You are learning how to use a new tool at more than a cursory level, and you are using this tool in new contexts, the information context and the subject context of your research question. The more you search, the better you will get at it.

Search Worksheet							
		1st keyword	OR	2nd keyword (synonym)	OR	3rd keyword (synonym)
	1st key concept	dogs	OR	cats	OR	pets
AND	2nd key concept	"mental health"				
AND	3rd key concept	"elderly ~~patients~~"				
AND	4th key concept	"nursing homes"	OR	hospitals		
Search Statement							
(dogs OR cats OR pets) AND "mental health" AND elderly AND ("nursing homes" OR hospitals)							

Figure 4.13: Revised Search Worksheet to Decrease Retrieval

Choosing Keywords

Choosing the right keywords, as you have just seen, is important to the success of your search. We usually pull our keywords directly from our research question. The following is our revised research question based on our successful search done earlier:

■ How does using dogs or cats or other pets with the elderly in nursing homes and hospitals impact their mental health?

You can see which keywords we chose to use in our search statement and also see which words were not chosen. "Impact" seems like a very important keyword that we did not use. Keywords represent a topic or subject or key concept. "Impact" is not a topic like "dogs" or "mental health." If we added "impact" to our search using an AND operator, because it represents a new key concept, it would cause the search to find fewer items. It would decrease retrieval. However, it would also decrease relevance, and this would have a negative impact on the success of our search statement.

"Impact" is not a good keyword, because it is not an essential descriptor of our topic. We cannot search for your topic without "dogs," "mental health," and "nursing homes," but we can search for it without "impact." If you use "impact" in your search, you will miss all the records that use the words "influence," "effect," "bearing," and "outcome" instead. Using "impact" limits your search, but not to an aspect of your topic, just to that word.

We have used synonyms in our search examples, and you already know that synonyms are words that mean the same thing. However, when searching for topics in a database, that definition is a little narrow. For our purposes, besides being words that have the same meaning, a synonym may be a similar or related topic. "Hospitals" is not a true synonym for "nursing homes," but it is an important, related topic. Synonyms should be a standard part of any search strategy. Not only will synonyms help you broaden your search and increase the amount of material you find, but one of those synonyms might turn out to be a better keyword than your original keyword.

Using Subject Searching and Field Searching

One field that you will find in the records in all commercial databases is the subject field. It may also be called the subject terms or descriptor field. No matter what it is called, the subject field is very important to conducting a good search. Search engines, by default, often search only a subset of the fields in a database. If you do not specify a field to search by choosing it from the drop-down box, then the predefined list is used. This is not a bad thing. The list of fields searched includes author, title, journal name, abstract, and subject. Depending on the database and the types of information in it, there may be a number of other fields that are included in the predefined search, like physical description, NAICS code, age group, gender, organism, and CAS registry number.

The information in the subject fields is provided by the creator of the database. A person called an indexer examines the articles to be included in the database to determine what the articles are about, then assigns subjects to the articles using a prescriptive list of approved subject terms called a thesaurus. A thesaurus of this nature is also called a controlled vocabulary because the indexer may only use the words on the list. These subject terms are added to the subject field of the record for each article.

If we do a quick, basic search for the keyword "fracking," as illustrated in Figure 4.14, we get about 4,000 results.

Our keyword was searched in the predefined fields, and it found 4,000 records that have the word "fracking" listed in at least one of its fields that were searched.

Fracking is slang, even though it is the most common way to talk about hydraulic fracturing. Hydraulic fracturing is the keyword phrase you will find in the subject field. If we want to search for hydraulic fracturing in the subject field, we will need to use the advanced search screen, and select "subject" from the drop-down list of fields.

| fracking | Search |

Figure 4.14: Basic Search for Fracking

	"hydraulic fracturing"	Subject ▼
And ▼		Fields ▼
And ▼		Fields ▼
		Search

Figure 4.15: Advanced Search for Subject Hydraulic Fracturing

Figure 4.15 illustrates our subject search. This search returned about 2,800 results. If we do a search using the predefined fields for "hydraulic fracturing," we retrieve 3,500 results which are right in the middle of previous two searches.

What is happening is that a standard search for fracking retrieves the most records because it is the most commonly used keyword for this topic, and it can show up in any field in the record. There could even be an author named Robert Fracking who writes on a completely different topic. Our standard search for hydraulic fracturing retrieved the second most records and more than the subject search for the same reasons that fracking retrieved the most. The search looked for "hydraulic fracturing" in all the predefined fields. That means the search could have found it in the title or abstract fields. The search of the subject field for "hydraulic fracturing" returned the fewest results because the search was limited to only that field in all the records.

However, that subject field search returned the most relevant results. The records retrieved and the articles they represent in a subject search are going to be about that topic. They are not going to have a passing mention or be tangentially related to the topic, but the topic will be a primary focus of the article. This is why you would want to do a subject search. The other benefit is that you will find all of the articles about a topic if you do a successful subject search.

For example, in a previous search, illustrated in Figure 4.13, we looked for the effects that dogs have on the mental health of patients. It took a few revisions to get the search to work well in the sense that it retrieved a manageable number of records. When you look closely at the records found, some of them are about the mental health of old dogs and cats, and other topics that are not related to what we wanted our search to find.

If we know that "therapy animals" is the official subject term for dogs and cats and all other animals used for therapy, we can eliminate the irrelevant results (Figure 4.16). However, the term is so specific the

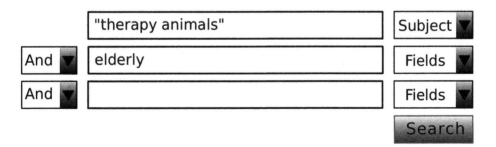

Figure 4.16: Complex Subject Search on an Advanced Search Screen

rest of the search needs to be modified as well to find these relevant results. Eliminating irrelevant records from your results takes more effort than it is worth. Reducing the number of irrelevant records and increasing the relevance of your results is good enough if you retrieve a manageable number of records. Using a subject search is a great way to improve the relevance of your search results, but there is a chance that you may need to reevaluate your whole search to take advantage of this type of search.

There are three ways to find subject terms to use in your searches. The first is to do a standard search using your keywords. Next, you examine your results and find a record that seems relevant to your search. Examine the subject terms of that record to see how it was indexed, and to find the official terms to use in a subject search, then revise your search using any or all of the subject terms while specifying the search to be done in the subject field. This sounds complicated and time-consuming but takes very little time. This is also a good habit to get into because it will help you evaluate and revise your search.

The second method is to look at the top of the database screen for any one of the following words: subjects, subject terms, index, headings, major concepts, and thesaurus. There are other possible names the listing of the controlled vocabulary used to assign subject terms. Medline, a very important database of medical journal articles, uses the term MeSH for its long-established thesaurus which stands for medical subject headings. If you do not see this term, you may need to explore any of the other options listed.

The third method is to guess. If we enter the keyword "fracking" on the advanced search screen and select the subject field from the drop-down list of fields, we should expect to find zero records. We know that fracking is not a subject term. However, since the database we happen to be using has a thesaurus, it tries to map common keywords to subject terms. In this case, we retrieve the same 2,800 records as our subject search for the official term "hydraulic fracturing." If our database did not support this kind of mapping, and we guessed wrong at a subject term, then we would have to use the first method.

When you limit your search to any specific field within the records of a database, you are performing a field search. Subject searching is a specific type of field searching. You can also limit your search to any of the other fields in a database. For example, if you know the author of an article or book you want to find, you can search for their name in the author field. The author's name is searched only in the author field, not in any of the other fields. This means that even if you search a common name like Williams, you are finding Williams only as an author, not as a subject or as a word in the title. This lowers the retrieval and increases the relevance of your search results.

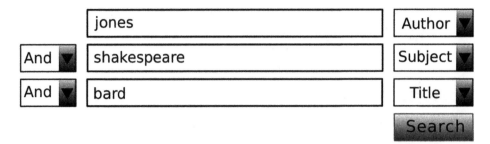

Figure 4.17: Complex Field Search on an Advanced Search Screen

Another useful field to search is the title field. If you know the title, using a title search finds exactly the information you want. If you remember bits of information for an individual item you want to find, then a field search may be the answer. Figure 4.17 illustrates a complex search using multiple fields.

This search returned the one record we were looking for.

Vocabulary

" "

( )

advanced search screen

AND operator

basic search

Boolean operators

controlled vocabulary

database

field

field searching

index

invisible web

keywords

nesting

NOT operator

OR operator

phrase searching

record

relevance

retrieval

search statement

stemming

stop words

subject searching

synonyms

Venn diagrams

visible web

Questions for Reflection

What is the difference between free and fee databases?

What is the difference between a basic and an advanced search?

What does each of the Boolean operators do?

How do you choose keywords?

What is a search statement?

How do double quotation marks work in a search?

What do parentheses do in a search?

Assignment

Open your research journal. Take your research question from Chapter 2, enter it on the Search Statement Worksheet, and pull out the keywords from your research question to build your first search (Figures 4.18 and 4.19). Do not use synonyms for this search. Your search should have three to four lines. Try your search in a general research database provided by your library. Record the name of the database and the number of items found. If you do not know what database to use, ask your librarian for help.

Examine the results of your first search and revise your search statement to improve the relevance of the records retrieved. This time, you should use at least one synonym for each of your key concepts, but do not use a field search. Again, your search should have three to four lines. Record the number of items found.

Examine the results of your second search and revise your search one last time. This time, use a subject search for one of your key concepts and keep your search to three or four lines. Record the number of items found.

Finally, examine all three searches, pick the one that worked best, and describe why it worked better compared to the other searches.

Research Question		
What specific effects do a lack of access to the Internet have on students' academic performance?		
Database Searched		
Academic Search Premier		
1st Search		
		keyword
	1st key concept	access
AND	2nd key concept	Internet

Figure 4.18: Search Statement Worksheet Example

AND	3rd key concept	students					
AND	4th key concept	"academic performance"					

1st Search Statement
access AND Internet AND students AND "academic performance"

Number of Records Retrieved	25

2nd Search

		1st keyword	OR	2nd keyword (synonym)	OR	3rd keyword (synonym)
	1st key concept	access	OR	use		
AND	2nd key concept	Internet	OR	web		
AND	3rd key concept	"high school students"	OR	teenagers	OR	adolescents
AND	4th key concept	"academic performance"	OR	grades	OR	scores

2nd Search Statement
(access OR use) AND (Internet OR web) AND ("high school students" OR teenagers OR adolescents) AND ("academic performance" OR grades OR scores)

Number of Records Retrieved	396

3rd Search

		1st keyword	OR	2nd keyword (synonym)	OR	3rd keyword (synonym)
	1st key concept	"academic achievement"	Field Name		subject	
AND	2nd key concept	access	OR	use		

Figure 4.18: (Continued)

AND	3rd key concept	Internet	OR	web		
AND	4th key concept	"low income"	OR	poor	OR	

3rd Search Statement
(access OR use) AND (Internet OR web) AND ("high school students" OR teenagers OR adolescents) AND "academic achievement" in Field Name=Subject

Number of Records Retrieved	16

Which search statement worked best and why did it compared to the other two? Be specific.
My first search retrieved a good number of records, but looking at them, they mostly didn't deal with my topic. This was very disappointing. I changed some of my keywords in my second search and added synonyms. I wasn't expecting it to find so many items! In my third search, I looked up the subject term for academic performance. It's academic achievement. I used that as the keyword for a subject search. I changed my last concept from students to "low income." I guess students is redundant when asking for academic achievement, but low income is what I really wanted, anyhow. And the search results are much more relevant to what I wanted. Most of them reflect my topic.

Figure 4.18: (*Continued*)

		1st keyword	OR	2nd keyword (synonym)	OR	3rd keyword (synonym)

Research Question

Database Searched

1st Search

		1st keyword	OR	2nd keyword (synonym)	OR	3rd keyword (synonym)
	1st key concept					
AND	2nd key concept					
AND	3rd key concept					
AND	4th key concept					

1st Search Statement

Number of Records Retrieved

2nd Search

		1st keyword	OR	2nd keyword (synonym)	OR	3rd keyword (synonym)
	1st key concept					
AND	2nd key concept					
AND	3rd key concept					
AND	4th key concept					

2nd Search Statement

Number of Records Retrieved

3rd Search

		1st keyword	OR	2nd keyword (synonym)	OR	3rd keyword (synonym)
	1st key concept		Field Name			
AND	2nd key concept					

Figure 4.19: Search Statement Worksheet

AND	3rd key concept					
AND	4th key concept					
3rd Search Statement						
Number of Records Retrieved						

Which search statement worked best and why did it compared to the other two? Be specific.

Figure 4.19: (*Continued*)

CHAPTER 5

Searching the Library Catalog and Evaluating Its Resources

In This Chapter

You will learn:

- What the library catalog is
- How to use the unique search environment of the catalog
- How to locate materials
- How to evaluate the materials you find
- How to utilize the materials you find

A library catalog is a database of all the materials a library owns that are available for customers to use. The format of the item does not matter. It could be a book, a painting, tools, an eBook, or a DVD. All of these items are in the catalog for you to find. Like all databases, the catalog is a record for each item in the library's collection. The fields in the records describe the items and help you find the materials you need.

Through a search of the catalog, you find the books that your library has shelved in the stacks and eBooks that are linked directly to the record for you to use. Catalogs also list the titles of journals that your library owns in print. However, to access the contents of the journals in order to find articles on a particular topic, you will need to use the commercial databases that your library provides. We will look at those databases in Chapter 6.

Searching the Library Catalog

Library catalogs have a very broad scope, and the depth of the material, the number of items they have on a particular topic, varies with the size and purpose of the library. The catalog will include primary and secondary sources. The primary sources will be book-length research, or books that contain primary sources like letters and photographs, and autobiographies. Most of the material will be secondary in nature. Books and background sources in digital or print formats will make up the largest percentage of the records in the database.

Library catalogs are small compared to commercial databases. Searching a small database requires you to think more about your search statement. You need to broaden your search to find materials relevant to your information need and research question. The nature of the materials in a library catalog also requires you to think in broad terms. A book is less likely to be as focused as your research question, and background sources are much broader than books. You will need to find materials that encompass your topic, and then find the information you need within them.

Your public library catalog may be very different from the catalog you use at school. However, all catalogs support a basic search and Boolean operators. Many have advanced search screens, as well. Library catalogs make it easy to do field searching because searching for a title, an author, or a subject is common in a library catalog. If you want to see whether your library owns a specific book, then a title search is fast and efficient. If you are looking for books by a certain author, then the author search is a better search than a keyword search. There are many different software options for library catalogs, but the basic functionality is the same. You may need to explore the catalog to find the advanced search screen, or there may be buttons below the search box for author, title, and subject searching that will execute your search in the corresponding field (Figure 5.1).

You do not have to enter a keyword into each search box but can pick and choose which ones you want to use. You can also use the drop-downs on the right-hand side to change the fields. If the item you are looking for has two authors and you know their last names, change the first search field to Author, and use two author lines to execute your search. You can also use AND within the Author search box to link your two authors together.

Figure 5.1: Catalog Advanced Search Screen

Subject field searching, as discussed in Chapter 4, is a little more difficult. The subject terms used to describe the materials in your library's catalog come from a thesaurus as they do with commercial databases. However, your catalog may not have a link to the thesaurus to help you find the right subject term. You will need to use the keyword search method covered in Chapter 4 to find relevant records whose subject terms you can then check. Subject field searching is a great way to find books or background sources about a person. If you are interested in information about an author as opposed to the books she wrote, then using a subject field search is the way to separate what she wrote from what has been written about her. For example, if you want books about J. K. Rowling, a subject search retrieves from our catalog 15 results, while an author search retrieves 53 results.

Many catalogs offer a browse feature. This allows you to browse through lists of authors, titles, subjects, and call numbers. To perform a browse search for subjects, you enter a keyword into the browse search box, and the result it retrieves is an alphabetical list of subject terms on either side of your keyword. You then browse up and down the list to find a subject term that fits with your research topic. Figure 5.2 shows a results list from a subject browse search of "Rowling."

1.	Rowley, William, 1585?–1642?--Oeuvres de collaboration.	1
2.	Rowling, J. K.	4
3.	Rowling, J. K.--Characters--Harry Potter.	6
4.	Rowling, J. K.--Criticism and interpretation.	8
5.	Rowling, J. K.--Film and video adaptations.	2
6.	Rowling, J. K.--Influence.	1

Figure 5.2: Subject Browse Search Results for Rowling

In the results list, you can see that the first entry is for Rowley. This is the closest alphabetical entry that comes before Rowling that our catalog has. There is one item about William Rowley's works. There are four items about J. K. Rowling, six about her Harry Potter characters, and eight that are critical analyses of her works. If you are unsure of your topic or if you will find anything, try a very broad subject browse search. In the example used in Figure 5.3, we used "nuclear" as our keyword to see what topics are available and how they are expressed.

Again, the first result is a subject term that immediately proceeds "nuclear." Our first subject term is "nuclear accidents," and there are two items in the library that are described with that term. If you want to know what those items are, click on the subject term, and you will see a results list with those two items. The next line is a cross reference; clicking on that will show you other possible subject terms to use in our search. If you are unsure of the spelling of an author's name or do not know the first name, if you want to see how many items your library has on a given subject, or if you want to see what is on the shelf in a specific area, these browse searches are very helpful.

Your library's catalog may have other search features that are designed to help you find what you need. For example, you may be able to limit your search to a type of material like DVDs, music, and eBooks. You may be able to limit your search to collections in the library like background sources or oversized books. If you need a book in French, you may also be able to limit your search by the language in which it is written. These limiters are also called facets. Facets can be used prior to or after your search is executed. Facets are additions you make to your search that do not change your search statement but instead add special conditions that your search needs to meet. The process is called limiting.

Your library's catalog may allow you to see what you have checked out and perform a renewal on any or all of those items with a click of

1.	Nuckolls County. Geology--Nebraska	1
2.	Nuclear accidents.	2
3.	see related headings for: Nuclear accidents	
4.	Nuclear aircraft carriers--United States--Design and construction.	1
5.	Nuclear arms control.	34
6.	see related headings for: Nuclear arms control	

Figure 5.3: Subject Browse Search Results for Nuclear

the mouse. It may allow you to place holds on items that are checked out, so you will be contacted as soon as that item is returned. It may let you keep lists of items you want to read and suggest books to purchase. Be sure to explore your catalog and see what features it has to offer.

Retrieving Materials

Call numbers are used to put physical materials on the shelves in order in many libraries. Call numbers order materials by subject. So when you copy down a call number and go to the shelves, not only should you find the item in which you were interested, but also any other items on that same topic. For example, all the DVDs on starting a small business will be next to each other because their call numbers will be the same. This system is designed to encourage browsing the shelves. Look to the left and right of the item you find and see what else your library might have.

Your library will have the books shelved by either Dewey Decimal Classification call numbers or Library of Congress Classification call numbers. The Dewey Decimal Classification system is often used in smaller libraries, public libraries, and schools libraries. The Library of Congress Classification system is designed for larger libraries. You will find it in use at most large public and academic libraries.

The Dewey Decimal Classification system divides knowledge into ten broad areas from 000 to 900. For example, the 100s are philosophy and psychology, the 300s are social sciences, and the 700s are arts and recreation. Within each area, there are many subcategories. For example, 770 is the number for photography. 778.9 is the number for nature photography.

Items are arranged on the shelves from low numbers to high numbers. Dewey makes that easy to understand. It is the decimal part of the call number that makes it. The sequence of decimal numbers here is in order from smallest to largest.

- .05, .1, .111, .12, .125, .13, .17, .2

For example, if your library had books with the numbers 569.6 and 569.74, the book numbered 569.6 would come first because it is the smaller number.

Library of Congress call numbers use letters and numbers to designate subjects. The broad categories include A for general works, B for philosophy, psychology, and religion, then skipping ahead, H is for social science and business, L is for education, P is language and literature, T is science, and so on. For a complete list of the Library of Congress classification, you can look at the Wikipedia article ("Library of Congress Classification" 2016).

Dewey Decimal Number	Library of Congress Call Number
577.2 .C36 2016	QH 325 .C36 2016

Figure 5.4: Dewey Decimal and Library of Congress Call Number for *The Big Picture*

A second letter is used to divide the topics into smaller categories, and then numbers on a second line divide those categories into even smaller subject categories. While B is the broad category of philosophy, psychology, and religion, BF177–176.5 is for psychological tests and testing, and BF180–198.7 is for experimental psychology. Those numbers are decimal numbers, just like in the Dewey system; that means a book with the call number BF 181.41 would come before a book with the call number BF 181.5.

Both Dewey and Library of Congress use Cutter numbers and year of publication to further identify a specific book. Cutter numbers are decimal numbers, too. So two books on exactly the same topic, but with different authors, would be next to each other based on the order of the Cutter number. The year of publication may be part of the call number, as well. It will distinguish different editions of a book from each other, besides showing you which books are the most current on your research question as you browse the shelves. The bigger the library, the more important the other numbers, besides the call number, are to finding the item. Figure 5.4 shows an example of a Dewey Decimal call number and a Library of Congress call number for the same book *The Big Picture* by Sean M. Carroll, which includes both a Cutter number and the year of publication.

Evaluating Sources Found through the Library Catalog

Evaluation, in general, means examining your work or the work of others and making an informed judgment, not based on opinion or belief, but supported by facts, about the quality of that work. Evaluation of information sources is a vitally important step in the research process.

When evaluating resources you find in the library catalog, you need to evaluate the quality of both the resource and the information it contains. The quality of your research project is directly affected by the quality of your research. If you use bad information as the basis of your research paper, then your research paper will also be bad. To avoid this, you need to evaluate the resources you find. We will use three main factors to examine the information, relevance, purpose, and validity. In this chapter, we will use these three factors to evaluate the materials you will find via a catalog search, which are books, eBooks, background sources, and videos. In the next two chapters, we will apply these factors to magazine articles, journal articles, and web pages.

Relevance

Relevance is the easiest of the three factors to evaluate. If you find a book that might be on your topic, you examine the book to find out if it does contain information on your topic that will help you with your research and answer your information need. If the answer is yes, then you have a relevant information source. If the answer is no, then the book or video is not relevant and should be eliminated from your pool of potential information resources.

For background sources, you will need to see if they contain entries on your topic or aspects of your topic. If they do, the information may be of the type that you do not want to use in your research, but may give you some important background information that gives you a better understanding of your topic and a better idea of potential keywords to use when you revise your search. This would make the background sources relevant. If they do not contain any information on your research question, then you need to find another background source.

Purpose

Purpose asks how much information is it trying to present, and why was this book written or this video produced?

Scope and Depth

We have previously talked about scope and depth. You will be happy to know that it still means the same thing in this context. If the item talks about the entirety of the Civil War in a 100-page book or a two-hour documentary, then its scope is necessarily very broad, and the depth is very shallow. If the item uses 600 pages or 12 hours to discuss the precursors of the Civil War, then you can expect narrower scope and greater depth.

Use this information about scope and depth to determine if this is the kind of information your research needs. You may want a paragraph from the broad resource to help introduce your topic, but your focus may closely align with the information in the resource that has greater depth.

Style

Some items are written to inform, to present information about a topic without overtly expressing or supporting a particular point of view. The information is allowed to speak for itself; the author or director is engaging in a form of reportage whether they conducted an original research project, or documented a volcanic eruption and its impact it had on the people who lived near it.

Other items are more like advertisements. They are written and produced to sell you something. In this case, it would be the ideas of the author or the opinions of the director. The information is carefully arranged, edited, and distorted to tell only the story the author wants to be told. There is no other possible interpretation allowed. It is not reportage. These items have a strong point of view that the author or director is trying to prove to you or get you to agree with. You do *not* want to use these items in your research. We will discuss more ways to spot this type of information in the section later on validity, but for now, be aware of items that do not let the material speak for itself or seem to be missing information.

Items aimed at a popular audience will have a more information style, and higher entertainment value. They want you to keep reading or watching, so they will try to present their information in a more engaging manner than a scholarly counterpart. They do this not necessarily to dilute their information but to expand its potential audience. A scholarly book on the same topic has other scholars or researchers as its audience. A scholarly book should have more value to your research question because it will directly reference information sources as they are used and have less anecdotal story-like first-person accounts.

Many books and documentaries are secondary sources that may contain some first-person, primary accounts. Unless your research is about a specific person, you want to be careful when using primary accounts about people or events as they are personal reflections, and as such, they may obscure the facts.

Validity

Validity is the most important factor in the evaluation. Validity is where you evaluate the truthfulness of the information source. There are many reasons why an information source may be more or less truthful.

Timeliness

Timeliness is the first part and easiest part of validity to evaluate. If an item is old, it may be less valid than a new item. It is the age of the material, and not necessarily the authors' intent to deceive. For example, things change quickly in medicine and astrophysics. A five-year-old book on cancer treatments and a seven-year-old documentary on the expanding universe will both have outdated information, that is, information that has been superseded by newer, more accurate information. In astrophysics, this older information will make you inaccurate. In medicine, this older information could harm you.

What is old is determined by the context of your research question, and whether the information has been superseded. For instance, a history book that is 20 years old may have not only the up-to-date information but may represent the best thinking ever done on the topic. However, if new information about the historical event came to light in the past two years, some or all of the information in the history book could now be out of date due to the new information.

Authority

Authority is also contextual. Here is a simple example of what that means. In Figure 5.5, each of the five authors has written a book with the same title.

The only difference seems to be in the authors' qualifications to write this book. What might be the difference in the scope and depth of the book by the reporter versus the books by the economics professors? How might style and purpose vary from the book by the librarian versus the book by the University of Chicago professor? Which book is the best one based solely on the authors' qualifications?

In answer to the last question, the University of Chicago is famous for its economics department which has won twelve Nobel Prizes ("Chicago School of Economics" 2016) and has 5 Nobel Prize winners currently on its staff (The University of Chicago 2016). Clearly, there is prestige in working at the University of Chicago, and this prestige translates to authority, especially in the field of economics.

Title of the Book	Author of the Book
Economic Theory and the Equitable Society	by a professor of early English literature
	by a librarian at a small college
	by a reporter at a national newspaper
	by a professor of economics at a mid-sized state school
	by a professor of economics at the University of Chicago

Figure 5.5: Information Context of a Book and Its Author

Not only does the institution worked for lend authority to an item, so does the publisher of the information. In Figure 5.6, we have added information about the publisher.

How does knowing this information about the publishers affect your opinions of the various books? What is the difference between a university press and a popular publisher, and how might that impact the quality of the information? Does knowing the publisher help in understanding how the style and validity factors may differ?

When evaluating a library resources for authority, you need to examine the authors and directors, their credentials, scholarly degrees, awards and recognitions, reviews of the item in question and other items they produced, what else they may have published or directed, and on what topics to help establish their authority on this subject. First, check the library catalog where you found the item. Are there any more items by the same author in your library that you can examine? Next, look for reviews of the item or other items by the same director in the library database and on the web. Read the author information provided in the book. Google the author or director and find information about them online. Develop a picture of who the creator of the item is, and a picture of the quality of the item will begin to emerge.

For book publishers and video producers, you need to examine what subjects they may focus on. A producer of video only about economics is likely to be more careful about his next economics video than a producer who does not specialize in any subjects. Publishers and producers have established reputations based on the quality of the material they produce. Oxford University Press has a better reputation for publishing quality materials than a no-name, small, midwestern publisher. Reputation is part of authority, but it is not a guarantee of quality. Find information about the publisher from its website and a web search.

Title of the Book	Author of the Book	Publisher of the Book
Economic Theory and the Equitable Society	By a professor of early English literature	Small university press
	By a librarian at a small college	Small popular publisher
	By a reporter at a national newspaper	Large popular publisher
	By a professor of Economics at a mid-sized state school	Large university press

Figure 5.6: Information Context of Book, Author, and Its Publisher

Accuracy

Accuracy is the most important factor to check, but it can be the hardest to determine. One very good way to do this is to fact-check. If the author says X, then check other sources to make sure X is true. For example, you are watching a video about colonizing Mars, and it states that the summer time, the equatorial average daytime temperature is a very pleasant 20°C. You can quickly and easily check this fact in a background resource. One background resource confirms this temperature but points out that the nighttime temperature in the same location at the same time of the year can be −73°C (Sharp 2012). Another background resource points out the overall average temperature on Mars is −63°C and that the lows at the poles in winter can be as cold as −140°C (U.S. Department of Commerce 2016). A third and final background resource indicates that temperatures range from 20°C to −140°C (Ridpath 2012). This background information comes from these three sources, respectively: Space.com, Weather.gov, *A Dictionary of Astronomy* published by Oxford University Press. So our source is not right. The daytime temperature at the equator can reach 20°C, but that is the daytime high, not the daytime average. Mars is generally cold.

Another check for accuracy is to see if the resource you find cites its sources of information. In other words, do they support their positions with factual information from another source? This means you may need to look up these cited sources, also known as the bibliography, to see if they are from scholarly sources, have qualified authors who are presenting facts, is published by a reputable publisher, and contains current, up-to-date information. Look at how many sources were cited. This is a good indication that the author or director did their homework. A book that is 600 pages long and cites only five sources is less likely to be accurate than a 200-page book that cites 100 sources. Look to see if the author cites the same source multiple times or if the author cites her own works multiple times. Overuse of self-citation is a red flag for validity.

Utilizing Library Resources

Once you have located the items from your library's catalog, you need to find and use the information within them. For a book, this may mean reading the whole thing, or using the table of contents or index. The index of any book will guide you to the entry or chapter where that keyword is mentioned. Use the table of contents to find a chapter or section of a book that relates to your research question. This will help you to find and read just the information you need. eBooks have a search feature that will take you right to a keyword in the text.

Background sources are designed for the quick look-up of information and are most frequently arranged alphabetically by topic, making them easy to use. If you cannot find the information you need, be sure to check the index. What you are looking for may not have its own entry, but may be part of another entry. Some digital background sources included multiple background information sources that are all searched at once. If the background source you are searching is like this, then be sure your keyword is the headword, the title of the entry in the results list. Otherwise, it may only be mentioned in an entry about another topic. A search of one publisher's collection of background sources had no articles with a headword "impact factor," but it did have 146 articles that talked about it. Another publisher's collection of background sources had three items with the headword "impact factor" that describe what an impact factor is, but only seven entries that mention impact factor. This is a good illustration of the need to use multiple resources to find the information you need.

When you are reading from a resource, be sure to take notes and summarize the information you find. If you come across a particular sentence or phrase that you really like, copy it verbatim so you can quote it in your research paper. You should note the page number where you found the quote and always copy the citation information for your source. You will need this information for your in-text citations and your bibliography.

How you take your notes is up to you. Most students prefer to use a laptop, but an interesting study says you are better off taking lecture notes longhand (Mueller and Oppenheimer 2014, 1161). This research says that by taking notes longhand, you will do better on tests of both your factual and conceptual knowledge. Because writing is slower than typing, you must process the information more when you take longhand notes. Processing the information means that you have begun the analysis of your information, already. There may be some carryover from lecture to notetaking from information sources, but the article does not address this. Using a laptop with eBooks and e-background sources makes sense. It makes taking a quote from an information source easy with the copy and paste functions. However, with this research study in mind, be sure to summarize and paraphrase the information you find because it will help you begin to analyze and synthesize the information you found.

You can use programs like EasyBib (http://www.easybib.com), EndNote (http://www.endnote.com), or Zotero (http://www.zotero.org) to records your citation information and manage all the information you found in your research. We will discuss managing information in more depth in Chapter 9.

Vocabulary

accuracy

agreement

author field search

authority

browse search

call number

citation

credentials

Cutter number

depth

Dewey Decimal Classification

entertain

fact checking

index

inform

library catalog

Library of Congress call numbers

persuade

purpose

relevance

reputation

scope

self-citation

style

subject field search

table of contents

timeliness

title field search

validity

Questions for Reflection

How is the library catalog different from other databases?

How do call numbers work?

How do an author's credentials impact the validity of a book?

Why would an eBook with a broad scope be a good potential information resource for your research?

How do you find information within a book, an eBook, or a video?

Which of the evaluation factors are the most important to evaluating library resources?

Assignment

Open your research journal; take your research question from Chapter 2 and enter it in the Catalog Search and Item Evaluation Worksheet (Figures 5.7 and 5.8). Find a background source that relates to your research question, and one book or eBook or video on your question. Record your search statement that found the material, and the call number, author, and title of the material.

Retrieve the material and examine it closely. Then using the three factors of evaluation, evaluate each source for quality. Be sure to address each aspect and give specific information about the resources that pertains to the factor. You may have to look up information about the author and the publisher, and you may want to find reviews for the material.

Finally, select which information source you are more likely to use in your research, and discuss why you choose it. Give specific reasons why you choose that item.

Research Question:		
How are biodiversity and extinction of species related to the health of the planet?		
Background Source Search Statement:		
biodiversity		
Call Number:	**Title:**	**Author:**
QH541.15.B56 E53 2013	Encyclopedia of biodiversity	Levin, Simon A
Background Source Evaluation		
Relevance:		
This source is very relevant to my topic, because it is about biodiversity and contains information on extinction, as well.		
Purpose:		
Scope and Depth		
Because it is an encyclopedia, it has a lot of scope, and since it is specialized, it also has pretty good depth.		
Style		
It is written to inform, and the style is neutral and scholarly. It does not advocate for a point of view. It just presents the information.		
Validity:		
Timeliness		
The background source is not too old. It was published in 2013. There are more extinct creates, now, but the effects of biodiversity on the planet's health should be the same, now.		
Authority		
The chief editor is Simon A. Levin who is a professor of ecology and evolutionary biology at Princeton university. He has written 20 books and 70 articles on the topic of biology and ecology. The publisher is Academic Press which publishes scientific information. It has been around for 70 years, and it is an imprint of Reed Elsevier which is one of the largest publishers of scholarly information in the world.		
Accuracy		
The entries seem to be accurate. Each entry has its own author who is an authority in the field, and each entry also has a bibliography. There are lots of tables and illustrations. The information I checked was the same in other sources.		

Figure 5.7: Catalog Search and Item Evaluation Worksheet Example

Grade:	A

Book Search Statement:		
biodiversity AND extinction		
Call Number:	**Title:**	**Author:**
HD60 .A287 2014	Accounting for biodiversity	Jones, Michael

Book Evaluation

Relevance:
Parts of this book directly address my topic, though the overall subject is about how business can promote biodiversity through their accounting methods.

Purpose:
Scope and Depth
This book is pretty narrowly focus, but does offer depth on the topic. It is 322 pages long.

Style
The style is informative, and it points out the benefits of biodiversity to the planet and business. There is an element of persuasion, but it is minor and supported by the research.

Validity:
Timeliness
This book was published in 2014, and it is pretty current. The topic has not changed much since then.

Authority
Michael Jones has written a few articles on accounting and the environment, but no other books. He is the head of the accounting department at the University of Bristol. This is kind of strange. The publisher is Routledge, and they are a leader in the humanities and the social sciences, which is where accounting and business fall.

Accuracy
Each chapter has an extensive bibliography.

Grade:	B

Selected Item and Why You Choose It:
I would use the Encyclopedia of Biodiversity. It more directly addresses my topic, and has multiple useful entries whereas the book only has some information, and that information is also in the encyclopedia. The articles in the encyclopedia are of moderate length and have lots of information, both background information and specific facts that I can use in my research.

Figure 5.7: (Continued)

Research Question:		
Background Source Search Statement:		
Call Number:	**Title:**	**Author:**
Background Source Evaluation		
Relevance:		
Purpose: Scope and Depth Style		
Validity: Timeliness Authority Accuracy		
Grade:		
Book Search Statement:		
Call Number:	**Title:**	**Author:**
Book Evaluation		
Relevance:		
Purpose: Scope and Depth Style		

Figure 5.8: Catalog Search and Item Evaluation Worksheet

Validity:	
Timeliness	
Authority	
Accuracy	
Grade:	
Best Item and Why You Choose It:	

Figure 5.8: (*Continued*)

Searching Library Databases and Evaluating Articles

In This Chapter

You will learn:

- How to choose a database
- How to use the unique search environment of commercial databases
- How to locate materials
- How to evaluate the materials you find
- How to utilize the materials you find

Your library's home page will direct you to the commercial databases that they license for you to use in your research. Your library may have only a handful of these costly resources, or it may have hundreds of commercial databases, and each database may contain tens of thousands or even millions of records. The first decision you need to make is deciding which one of those databases to search for information on your research question.

Choosing a Database

Your library will have a general database, that is, a database with a broad scope and information resources in all subject areas. Academic Search Premier is an example of a general database. It may be highlighted or featured on your library's web page. A general database is a good place to start your research. You can try out your search statement, find some relevant articles that will help you identify other, better keywords and subject terms, narrow the focus of your research, and perhaps even find enough good information for your research project.

If you do not find enough information in a general database, then you will have to try a subject-specific database. These are databases that focus on a specific field of knowledge or subject discipline. There are databases for every subject area, biology, literature, psychology, business, and everything else. If you are searching for information on frogs and climate change, then you will want the biology database like BioOne. If you are looking for anthropomorphic frogs in fiction, then you will want to use the literature database like MLA International Bibliography. Finally, if you are looking for the fear of frogs, you will want to search the psychology database like PsycINFO. Your library's web page has a list of these resources and may have organized that list of databases by subject with a brief description of what is contained within each database. This information will help you pick an appropriate database for you to search. If you do not find a list with descriptions, do not hesitate to ask the librarian for help picking a database. He knows the collection and what will work best for your research.

Your library may also have something called federated searching. Federated searching executes your search in multiple databases at the same time. Not all libraries have federated searching, and it may not be called that on your library's web pages. It may be a search box labeled "Find Articles" or "Search for Journal Articles in Multiple Databases." In cases like this, a predetermined subset of the library's databases will be searched. You may also be able to choose other predefined collections of databases to search which are grouped by subject.

Some vendors offer a form of federated searching. EBSCOhost calls it integrated search in its databases, while ProQuest does not give the feature a name in its. You can pick and choose which database to search or search all of the databases that your library license from that one vendor. This can be a substantial number and provide you an opportunity to search across many disciplines. You may have to look for this option on the search screen, and it may be under a label like "Databases" or "Choose Databases."

For federated searching to work with multiple databases from multiple vendors, it can only use the most basic search features. In that regard, federated searching typically supports Boolean operators, phrase searching, and field searching in common fields, like author and title. It does not support proximity operators because there is no standard for their implementation. Federated searching can be confusing to use because of feature differences, how results are displayed, and the large amount of records that it might find. Like any database search, you receive a results list that you can browse.

There is an additional piece of information on this results list. It is the name of the database where the item was found. This is another advantage of a federated search. You can do a quick and simple search for a topic, and discover which database contains the most information. Then you can directly search that database using your complex search and all the features the search engine has to offer. Federated searching is another tool that your library has to offer and one that is worth exploring.

Abstract and Full-Text Databases

Another thing to be aware of when choosing a database is the types of information it provides. There are three categories of databases based on the information they contain. They are abstract-only databases, full-text databases, and hybrid databases. An abstract-only database is the least desirable of the three categories, but it is still useful. In an abstract-only database, the results you retrieve will provide the full citation information, like the author, title, and publication information. An abstract, or short summary of the article, is provided, but there is no full text of the whole article available. Even though the full text of the article is not available, you would still choose to use an abstract-only database because it is the best database for your topic. Plus, there are ways to get the full text of the items you find.

Your library may have something called a link resolver which is a separate piece of commercial software that is added to the database software. Link resolvers add a line and/or an icon to each record that shows on the results list. It may have names like "full-text finder," "locate full-text," "check other databases," or "link to full-text." By clicking on the link resolver for items from which you need the full text, the link resolver checks all of the other databases your library licenses to see if that item is available in full text in another database. If it is, a link to that item is provided. If it is not, a link to your library's interlibrary loan system may be provided as a means to retrieve the full text of the item. Interlibrary loan was discussed in more depth in Chapter 3.

Full-text databases are those that have the full text for every item or record in the database. There are a handful of true full-text databases. License agreements between the database producer and the information producer make it difficult for any database to be truly full text, as there are some information producers who do not want the full text of their information to be available in a database. There are exceptions. For example, if your library purchased an eBook collection, then all the books in that collection should be full text. Most databases are hybrids. They contain a percentage of full text, with the remaining percentage of records having only abstracts. The percentage of full text will vary in each database, but vendors try to get the full text of the most commonly used journals and magazines giving you a better chance of finding the information you want in the database.

Searching Commercial Databases

Commercial databases support all the different search commands and options discussed in Chapter 4. That means they support Boolean operators, phrase and proximity search, nesting, and field searching, among others. The subject coverage of the database allows the database producer to include specific fields. For example, Business Source Premier allows a field search by North American Industrial Classification Number, better known as a NAICS code.

Figure 6.1 shows a NAICS code field search combined with the keyword "marketing." The NAICS code 312111 stands for soft drink manufacturers. You can find NAICS codes in many places, like NAICS.gov which will direct you to the NAICS code site at the Census Bureau. This search, then, finds all mentions of marketing that are related to the soft drink industry. Another unique field in business databases is the ticker symbol. You can search for a company by its stock exchange symbol.

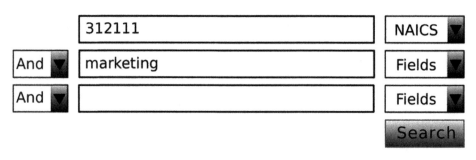

Figure 6.1: NAICS Code Search on Advanced Search Screen

Figure 6.2 illustrates a search using the ticker symbol field. The search is looking for either Coca-Cola (KO) or Pepsi-Cola (PEP) and their marketing to teenagers.

Commercial databases also implement facets to limit your search results that are similar to what we saw in library databases in the previous chapter. Some facets can be applied prior to your search. These facets are listed below the advanced search box. However, it is better to apply facets after the search has been executed. This is more flexible and allows you to see the effect any one facet is having on your search results and remove a facet that is too limiting. Figure 6.3 shows a list of facets compiled from multiple databases.

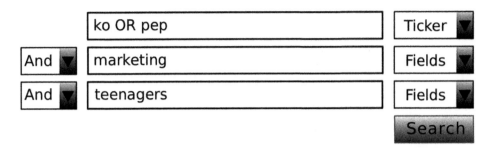

Figure 6.2: Ticker Symbol Search on Advanced Search Screen

Limit To
- ☐ Full-Text
- ☐ Books
- ☐ Conference Papers
- ☐ Dissertations
- ☐ Fossil
- ☐ References Available
- ☐ Reports
- ☐ Scholarly (Peer Reviewed) Journals

Publication Date

Source Types
- ☐ All Results
- ☐ Academic Journals
- ☐ Magazines
- ☐ Newspapers
- ☐ Reviews
- ☐ Trade Publications
- ☐ Wire Feeds

Age

Classification

Company

Document type

Gender

Geography

Language

Figure 6.3: Table of Facets

Methodology
NAICS/Industry
Population
Publisher
Subject
Tests and Measures

Figure 6.3: (*Continued*)

Limit To and Source Types have been expanded to show the options available. You can click on any of the facet names to see what the options are for that particular facet. There are many types of facets that will allow you to focus your results to very specific items. For example, the Methodology facet limits your results to articles that use a specific research method in their study. To apply a facet, simply click the box next to the facet you want. To remove a facet, click on the box, again.

Publication Date is an important facet. It allows you to select a date range, like 2002 to 2004, which is useful if you think the item you want to find was published in that range. Also, you can limit the date to items published before a specific date to find older information, or to items published after a specific date to limit the results to only the most current years.

The Full-Text facet is also a good choice, and it is very commonly used. It finds the information that is available right now in the database that you are searching. This is very useful when you do not have much time to get your research done. However, it does have drawbacks. You may miss a very good article that, while not full text in the database you searched, is full text in another database your library has or is available quickly through interlibrary loan. Be careful when selecting full-text–only searches and realize that you might be missing some good, relevant articles.

Limit To and Source Types overlap, but look closely to find the important differences, and remember that the facets available to you will be different in each database. You may select as many facets as you want to apply to your search results. If you check Full-Text and Magazines, you are limiting your search results to popular magazine articles that are available in full text in the database you are using. Another typical use of facets is to check Full-Text and Scholarly Journal or Academic Journal. This limits your results to full-text articles from scholarly journals. It is important to note that this does not limit your results to scholarly full-text articles. What this means is your search may have found a full-text editorial or a news piece in a scholarly journal. Neither of these are scholarly articles, but they are typically found in scholarly journals.

Evaluating Articles

This is an example of why evaluation of articles is important. You find a relevant item in a scholarly journal that you used in your report, but you do not get full credit for it because the item you found was a news piece or an interview, and not the scholarly article your instructor wanted. Another common mistake is assuming that since you search a commercial database and not the Internet, you found a good quality, reputable item, but using a commercial database is not a guarantee of quality resources. They contain thousands of sources and hundreds of thousand items. Not all of them can be good. This is why you still must evaluate the information you found. We will use the same three factors to evaluate database items, particularly articles.

Relevance

Relevance is, again, very easy to evaluate. Because this is an easy and fast evaluation that eliminates items from your potential pool, this evaluation factor should be applied first. If the articles you found address some aspects of your research question, they are relevant. Later, as you start to organize your thoughts and outline your research project, you will reevaluate the materials for relevance to your project, discarding the items that no longer fit in with your outline, or that you are not going to use.

Purpose

Commercial databases contain all types of materials that range widely in quality and in purpose. Some are intended to entertain, others to inform, some to educate, and still others to do all three. There is nothing wrong with an article that is both entertaining and informative as long as the information it presents is accurate and not biased.

Scope and Depth

A magazine article may act as a good background source for current events and discoveries, filling a gap that background sources are not timely enough to cover. It can provide an introduction to the subject, the names of the major players, and ideas for more avenues to explore. Its scope may be broad or focused on one event. It may cover an event with depth, especially if it is a cover story or a featured article.

A scholarly journal article on the same event may have an even narrower focus and greater depth and detail. Scholarly articles often follow a generic outline that includes a literature review. A literature review is a summary of the findings of other articles on the same or similar topic. This section adds more scope to a journal article, giving you an overview of the research that has already been done on the topic and the findings from this earlier research. This is an invaluable way to find more information on your topic. It is tempting to read the abstract of a scholarly article, and then skip to the conclusion but the literature review section of a highly relevant article can be a great asset in your research.

Style

Popular magazine articles use a vocabulary that most people can understand. This is what makes them a great place to start your research and learn something about an unfamiliar subject. However, you are more likely to encounter a biased point of view in a popular magazine article. It could be a subtle promotion of products advertised in the magazine to the blatant encouragement to buy a specific item. There may be bias by omission. A magazine that accepts advertisements from makers of assault rifles is unlikely to run an editorial that supports a ban on their sales. The magazine has a monetary interest in not supporting that point of view. This is a conflict of interest.

A magazine article may present multiple points of view but favor one over another. This could be the case but then all the information needs to be provided to show why that position is considered better than the others. If no information is presented to support the article's conclusions or the language used is biased and inflammatory, then the article has a stronger interest in promoting its point of view than presenting balanced arguments supported by facts.

Scholarly articles use the jargon of the discipline to communicate ideas to researchers and scholars in the field. This vocabulary requires some knowledge of the field to fully understand. The scholarly style is direct and the language neutral. Some would even call it flat, colorless, and boring. Scholarly articles use in-text citations and have bibliographies at the end of the article. Unfortunately, this is an easy format and style to imitate. It is easy to muddy the meaning or intent of a so-called scholarly article with jargon and poor citations. A scholarly article may use so much jargon that it is difficult to read and decipher its meaning. A scholarly article may be biased and trying to convince you of its point of view by using subtly biased language and bad citations. You will have to examine the language used in a scholarly article more closely to determine if that is the case. Format does not validate a scholarly article.

Validity

The peer-review process and the publisher do not validate an article, either. While these things do act as checks and balances, they do not guarantee quality. A publisher can create a scholarly journal with a biased peer-review process and only publish materials that support its point of view, then make the claim to scholarship. Reputable publications with strong, unbiased peer reviews can make mistakes. The greatest mistakes in scholarly publishing may be the publication in *Journal of Electroanalytical Chemistry* of an article by researchers Fleischmann and Pons that claimed that they had succeeded in creating a sustainable cold fusion reaction that would promise unlimited and cheap power. Because of the importance of the claim, and the climate of the times, this article was published without due diligence and its claims were quickly proven to be false ("Cold Fusion" 2016).

Timeliness

Timeliness asks if the information you found is up to date. Magazine and journals contain up-to-date information. Make sure your research captured enough information that there is agreement as to what current information looks like for this topic. You also need to check the dates of the cited information in the bibliographies of the information you are evaluating. For example, two articles look identical. They were both published recently in scholarly journals. They cover the same topic, have the same number of pages, and the same number of references in their bibliographies. When you look closely at the bibliographies, however, you notice that one of the articles cites only older sources with nothing being less than 10 years old. The citations in the other article's bibliography have a mix of dates, but the majority of references are to resources that are less than 10 years old. Clearly, the article based on more recent material meets the timeliness factor the best.

Authority

When evaluating the authority of magazine and journal articles, you use the same critical thinking skills that we talked about for evaluating books, videos, and background sources in Chapter 5. There are some differences, however. First, we do not expect that newspaper and magazine articles are written by Ph.D.s in the field. We expect them to be written by skilled reporters. Oftentimes, news pieces do not list the name of the author. This does not mean that the piece is inaccurate or badly written. It usually means that the piece is short and did not require the high level of research, involvement, and investigation to produce as longer, signed pieces. Some reporters in specific subject areas do have a credential in the field. Science and business reporters may have degrees in a subfield like biology and management, respectively.

Reporters need to keep the identity of their sources private in order to get information from them. This can cause problems because we are not able to identify the motives and accuracy of the sources of information. Good reporters will confirm the information with another source. However, even highly reputable publishers can make mistakes and let stories through that have not been confirmed and whose sources are suspect. This is why you should always confirm the information you are considering using in your research project in another source.

Research articles in scholarly journals are written by subject experts. When all the authors have Ph.D.s, it is difficult to evaluate authority. You can check to see if the author of an article has a publishing track record. In other words, what else have they published, how much, and in what fields? In the database where you found the record for the article you are evaluating, you can click on the author's name in the full records and this will execute an author search for that name. Look closely at the results. If your author is named John Smith, there are going to be plenty of other people with that name or with variations on that name. Some journals only use initials for first and middle names to make identifying your author more difficult. You need to check the subject of the articles to see if they are in the same field as your initial article. If your search was for frogs in the Amazon, and the author of the article was named Albertina P. Lima, then a click on her name is going to get you much better results.

If the author has written only one article, that does not mean that you should not use it. It means you should confirm the information in other sources, and place more emphasis on other aspects of the evaluation, like accuracy.

Accuracy

The scholarly publishing process does not guarantee quality. This is why it is important to read the methodology section of scholarly articles to help establish accuracy. You may not understand completely what the researchers are doing but use the common sense test. The research method that is used by the research has an impact on what kinds of conclusions can be made. If an interview method was used to promote the benefits of a drug, then the wrong method was employed and the methodology does not pass the common sense test. If researchers use a data set that includes only ten records, they cannot make broad, sweeping conclusions and claim these ten records represent thousands of cases. If a survey question presents one possible answer as the better choice than any of the other possible answers, then the survey has bias and the results will not be accurate. If researchers surveyed female high school students about how likely they are to buy a new luxury car from a specific automaker in the next year, then maybe the wrong group of people were surveyed. If the data say one thing, and the conclusion says another, then the research does not support the researchers' claims. Read the methodology section and see if it passes the common sense test.

Examining the citations and bibliographies of scholarly articles is another way to check on the accuracy of an article. We have already mentioned the age of the materials cited in the bibliography. This time, you are looking at the types of information cited, how much information is cited, who is cited, how it is used, and the quality of the information cited. That is a lot, but it is easier to do that it sounds. Here is a list of possible problems with citations and bibliographies and why it may be a problem (Figure 6.4). These things may not be problems depending on the context of the use of the citation.

When citations are used appropriately, they illuminate the topic and support the author's reasoning. Even an article with a contradictory point of view can be incorporated into a research paper to show the power of your reasoning and research or be used to show old, superseded thinking on the topic. Figure 6.5 shows some of the

Problem	Reason
• Ignoring contradictory information	• Possible bias and lack of confidence in own research
• Information from disreputable sources	• Poor research or possible bias
• Overreliance on one article	• Little else supports the research
• Overuse of self-citation	• Self-promoting and possible bias
• Short bibliography	• Did not do comprehensive research
• Too much information from popular sources	• Missing research perspective
• Too much information from secondary sources	• Research did not find enough scholarly articles
• Too much old information	• Does not reflect current state of knowledge

Figure 6.4: Citation and Bibliography Problems

Benefit	Reason
• Citation used appropriately	• Supporting arguments with right type of material
• Emphasis on current publication dates	• Aware of current state of knowledge
• Inclusion of contradictory information	• Confident in research and conclusions
• Many citations	• Comprehensive research
• Use of reputable sources	• Identification of quality sources
• Variety of sources	• Broad search
• Wide range of publication dates	• Knowledge of history and development of ideas

Figure 6.5: Citation and Bibliography Benefits

benefits from good citations and their proper use. Keep in mind that this is contextual and there are no hard and fast, right and wrong answers.

What if you are reading a scholarly journal article that talks about aspects of Romeo's character from Shakespeare's *Romeo and Juliet*, how do you check the facts? This is not a scientific article in the sense that an experiment was conducted. There are no charts presented and no methodology. How can this type of scholarly article be supported by facts? The facts, in this case, come from the text of the play. If the article states that Romeo speaks with a French accent, is very tall, and has a long, red beard, then you should be able to find mentions of all three of these statements in play, and they should be cited by the author of the article.

Utilizing Electronic Sources

Databases have many features to help you use the information you found. You can print, save, or e-mail an article of interest. Links to these features are at the top or on the right-hand side of the results list and the individual record display. Databases allow you to mark records which create a set of records that you can save, print, or e-mail all at once. If the records you found include full text, then when you choose a method to save the records, the full text will be included. To use these features, look for check boxes or a folder icon by each record to mark it.

Then click on the folder icon at the top of the screen to get to the list of your marked items.

Another feature databases offer is a citation generator feature. When you send or print your marked records, you can include a citation for it. You can also click on the cite link for an individual record and get the citation that way. You are given your choice of a few different citation styles and can pick the one that your instructor requires. You can use this feature to produce a bibliography of all your marked items. When you choose to print, e-mail, or save your marked items, you will be asked in what citation format you want the items. Pick a format, and a bibliography of those items will be included with the other material it is providing you. Be careful when using this feature. Databases do not always produce good, accurate citations. If the information is bad going in, it is bad coming out. You will learn what an accurate citation looks like in Chapter 9.

These features are very helpful, but as soon as you close the database, it will forget everything you did. Many databases offer services that will allow you to save your marked items in a personal account, so you can return to them later. You need to register for this service, but it is free and adds a number of other features like saving your search statements to execute later. They can even run your search automatically on a schedule you set to update your search results. One other feature you often find is a journal alert feature. Every time a new issue of a journal comes out that you selected for an alert, you get the table of contents sent to you, and if it is full text, you will get links to the full articles. This is a great way to browse the contents of magazines and journals you frequently read.

Of course, full-text databases make it easy to copy and paste quotes into your note-taking or word processing software. Doing this ensures that you will have the wording exactly right. Be sure to include the citation and page number with your notes and quotes.

Vocabulary

abstract-only databases	hybrid databases
bibliography	journal alert
citation	link resolver
common sense test	literature review
facets	marked records
federated searching	methodology
full-text databases	publishing track record
general database	subject-specific database

Questions for Reflection

Why would information producers not want the full text of their information to be available in a database?

What is federated searching?

Where is the listing for databases on your library's website?

How do you get an MLA citation for an article from a particular database?

What are the differences between a good magazine article and a good journal article?

How does the reputation of the publisher and the peer-review process affect the validity of a journal article?

Assignment

Open your research journal; take your research question from Chapter 2, and enter it in the Database Search and Item Evaluation Worksheet (Figures 6.6 and 6.7). Record the name of the database you are searching, and the number of results found in your successful search statement that retrieved between 20 and 80 results. You may have to adjust your search to find an appropriate number of items.

Find two full-text magazine articles and two full-text journal articles that you would consider using in your research on your topic. You cannot evaluate an article unless it is full text. Mark the four items you are going to use, and then use the database's citation feature to generate a bibliography of the items. Copy and paste this bibliography into your paper. Choose the magazine article and the journal article that you think are the best and evaluate both of them using the three factors. Finally, pick the best source of information between your magazine and journal article, and describe why you think it is the best choice for your research project.

Research Question: Does plagiarism help students do better academically?	
Database Searched:	Academic Search Premier
Search Statement and Number of Records Found: plagiarism AND academic achievement, 43.	

Figure 6.6: Database Search and Item Evaluation Worksheet Example

Bibliography from Database:	

References

Griffin, D. J., Bolkan, S., & Goodboy, A. K. (2015). Academic Dishonesty Beyond Cheating and Plagiarism: Students' Interpersonal Deception in the College Classroom. *Qualitative Research Reports In Communication, 16*(1), 9–19. doi:10.1080/17459435.2015.1086416

Cooper, J. (2007). PATCHWORK PLAGIARISM. *Knowledge Quest, 35*(4), 62–65.

Replicating success. (2010). *Economist, 396*(8692), 43.

Varadarajan, T. (2012). Schadenfareed. *Newsweek, 160*(9), 5.

Best Magazine Article Title:	Replicating Success

Evaluation of Best Magazine Article

Relevance: This is very relevant to my research because it's about students cheating in China.

Purpose: Scope and Depth This is a short article that talks in general terms about plagiarism and cheating in schools and among people in China. It is very broad, and has little depth. Style The style is to inform. There is no bias.

Validity: Timeliness It is 6 years old. That not new, but it isn't bad considering the topic. Authority There is no author, but it is reporting and it is from a reputable publication, The Economist. Accuracy It appears to be accurate, and I have found other articles that confirm this information.

Grade:	B
Best Journal Article Title:	Academic Dishonesty Beyond Cheating and Plagiarism: Students' Interpersonal Deception in the College Classroom.

Figure 6.6: (*Continued*)

Evaluation of Best Journal Article
Relevance: This article is exactly what I was looking for. It talks about why students plagiarize.
Purpose: Scope and Depth This article is pretty narrowly focused, but it has a lot of depth on my topic. Style This is a research article that reports results of a study. Its purpose is to inform and present facts.
Validity: Timeliness This is the most current article I found. The information is very up-to-date. Authority The authors are all PhD and work at different universities in departments of communications. They have written many articles on related topics, but nothing else on plagiarism. This should not be a problem because of their publishing track record. Accuracy The article has 21 citations to scholarly journals and books with dates ranging from 1989 to 2014. Most of the sources are current. This looks like very good research.

Grade:	A

Best Article and Why You Choose It: The journal article is the best. It is really relevant to my topic, has lots of information and depth, and is a very valid information source. The popular magazine article does not have any depth, and shows that plagiarism and cheating are a problem, but it only hints at why it's a problem. The journal article tells what students expect to get by cheating, and why it is important to them.

Figure 6.6: (Continued)

Research Question:	
Database Searched:	
Search Statement and Number of Records Found:	
Bibliography from Database:	
Best Magazine Article Title:	
Evaluation of Best Magazine Article	
Relevance:	
Purpose: Scope and Depth Style	
Validity: Timeliness Authority Accuracy	
Grade:	
Best Journal Article Title:	
Evaluation of Best Journal Article	
Relevance:	
Purpose: Scope and Depth Style	

Figure 6.7: Database Search and Item Evaluation Worksheet

| **Validity:** Timeliness

Authority

Accuracy	
Grade:	
Best Article and Why You Choose It:	

Figure 6.7: (*Continued*)

Searching the Web and Evaluating Websites

In This Chapter

You will learn:

- How web search engines work
- How to construct a good web search statement
- What advanced search features are available to use
- What a metasearch engine is
- How to evaluate information found on the open web

There is a lot of good information, and there is a lot of bad information available to everyone on the open web. Internet search engines like Bing and Google are easy to use, work well, and are incredibly fast especially since they index billions of web pages. However, they cannot evaluate all that information for you, and since the Internet is open to all who wish to create a web page with no review of the contents of any kind, evaluation is of paramount importance.

Web Search Engines

We are all familiar with the simple search box that Internet search engines present us. A lot of technology hides behind that search box to help you find the two or three good web pages on a subject out of the billions of pages that are indexed. Web search engines need to find web pages and index them to make them available for you to search. To do this, they use software programs called bots or spiders to crawl the web. A bot can essentially start on any web page and follow the links on that page to other pages, then follow the links on those other pages to more and more pages to find new or updated pages to index and include in their search engine's database.

When you use a web search engine, the first thing to know is that it uses the Boolean AND operator between your keywords. We call this an implied AND because you do not have to enter it into your search statement. Figure 7.1 compares an advanced search in a commercial database to a web search that works in exactly the same manner.

The preceding search found a little over 100 items in a general database but found between 180,000 and 280,000 items from web search engines. This is why relevancy ranking is such an important feature of web search engines. No one can sort through 100,000 records to find 2 or 3 good websites. Internet search engines use algorithms to develop a relevancy ranking for each record in the results list. Google's algorithm examines 200 factors to develop its page rank ("How Google Search Works—Search Console Help" 2016). Algorithms count how many times your search terms appeared on each page and where they appeared on the page, like in the title or in the headings. The algorithm also checks to see how many other pages link to the page it is ranking. The more links to it that a page has, the higher its rank. All this information for all the results is assigned a value, added up by the algorithm, and then the results are displayed in order by the most relevant page to the least.

One other thing that web search engines do is track your search behavior. This may not matter at school where the computers may wipe away your search profile every time you log out. It does matter on your personal computers and devices. They do this to show you advertisements for items you recently searched. This is not a bad thing, in itself. However, they also use your profile they have developed from your

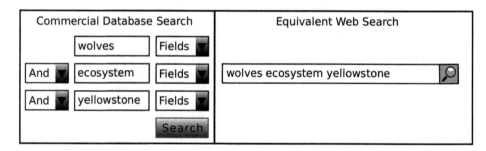

Figure 7.1: Advanced Commercial Database Search and the Equivalent Web Search

search history to customize your search results. Two people who enter the same search will not get the same search results (Tavani 2014). This shows a bias toward information that fits best with your personal profile as opposed to the sites with the highest ranking. You need to be aware that bias could be influencing the results of your search statement. To avoid this, you may want to use one browser like Chrome for your personal searching and another like Firefox for your research. You may also want to use a search engine like DuckDuckGo (https://duck duckgo.com/) that does not track your searches and modify the search results based on your profile.

Searching the Web

You can type anything into a web search box, including your entire research question, and you will get results. Some of these might even be good! With such a huge pool of information to draw from, it is important that you have a focused topic and multiple key concepts. The phrase operator is extremely important to use with your keyword phrases. It will decrease the number of results found and increase their relevance.

The example in Figure 7.2 illustrates the different search results achieved with different search statements, but the numbers only tell part of the story. Bing results are the same with and without the use of the phrase operator. However, if you look at the results list, you will see different results. The relevancy ranking has changed the order of the items on the results list based on the use of the phrase operator. The phrase operator made a significant difference in the number of results Google returned, and the items on that results list appear to be more relevant and of higher quality. Our searches with the full research question returned the most results in our Google searches and the least results in our Bing searches. The results of both searches were the least relevant and included the fewest quality sources.

Search Statement	Bing Results	Google Results
What effect do therapy animals have on the mental health of elderly patients in nursing homes?	4,350,000	1,200,000
therapy animals mental health nursing homes elderly patients	19,400,000	659,000
"therapy animals" "mental health" "nursing homes" "elderly patients"	19,400,000	967

Figure 7.2: Variations on a Search Statement and Web Search Results

You need to explore and experiment with your search statement to get the best results from web search engines. You may also need to take advantage of advanced features.

Advanced Searching

Bing and Google both support advanced search commands. These are like facets in commercial databases. Figure 7.3 is an example of one of these search commands.

This search specifies that the keywords need to be found on web pages that come from .edu sites. Like facets, these search commands reduce the number of items retrieved and limit the results to the specified facet, in this case by as much as 75 times fewer results, but unlike facets, they need to be applied before the search. Domains with .edu for educational sites and .gov for government sites are the two best domains for differentiating where the items come from. The other domains, like .com, .org, and .net, have lost their distinctiveness and blurred their meanings.

There are other commands that can be applied to your searches in this manner. For example, you can use a facet that will limit your search results to Excel files, ext:.xlsx. You will need to find a list of these commands on the web, like this one for Bing: http://onlinehelp .microsoft.com/en-gb/bing/ff808421.aspx.

Google does have an advanced search screen that makes it easier to apply these types of commands to your search. Unfortunately, it is no longer linked from the search results screen. You need to go directly to this address: https://www.google.com/advanced_search. On this screen, you get a number of search boxes that will help you construct a more precise search. Using a variation of our search from above, we will enter our keywords in the first search box. This box is equivalent to the basic search box. We will enter "music" into the "none of these words" box because we are not interested in this aspect of the topic. We will enter ".gov" into the "site or domain" box to limit our search to just .gov sites. Next, using the drop-down menu for the "terms appearing" box, we will select "in the title of the page" which is like a title field search, limiting our keyword to titles of web pages. Once we execute the search, we see the basic search box at the top of the results list with the advanced commands included (Figure 7.4).

copyright ethics site:.edu	🔍

Figure 7.3: Advanced Search Command in Web Search Engine

allintitle: copyright ethics -music site:.gov

Figure 7.4: Google Search with Advanced Commands

Seeing how the commands are applied will make it easy to skip the advanced search screen and use the advanced commands directly in the basic search box. The "-" used in front of a word is the Boolean equivalent of the NOT operator.

There are some facets that can be applied from the basic search results screens. These include "images" and "videos" that limit your search to these types of materials, and "news" that limits your search results to news stories on your topic. You can also limit the date the item was published by selecting a predefined range of time, like the last 24 hours, or supplying a date range of your own. All of these facets can be very helpful.

Remember that while relevancy ranking and advanced search commands are a great help in retrieving relevant results, it is not a guarantee that the search found good, reliable information. You still need to evaluate the information you find. We will talk about how to do this later in this chapter.

Metasearch Engines

Metasearch engines execute your search statement in more than one Internet search engine at a time. This is the web search counterpart to the federated search available for commercial databases. A metasearch engine executes your search in multiple web search engines at the same time. Dogpile (http://www.dogpile.com) is an example of a metasearch engine that you can find by searching for metasearch engines in your favorite search engine. Dogpile executes your search in Google, Yahoo!, and other web search engines (InfoSpace 2016).

It seems unnecessary to use a metasearch engine because Google indexes so many sites. However, if you try your search in different web search engines and compare the results, you will find unique items from each search engine due to differences in the indexes, and search and relevancy ranking algorithms. You can easily compare results lists using a web search page like CompareWebSearch (http://com parewebsearch.com) which searches Google, Bing, and Yahoo! at the same time, but displays the results in three side-by-side windows. The Search Ranking Comparison Tool from Shrink the Web (http://www .shrinktheweb.com/content/search-results-rankings-comparison.html) allows you to compare the results of a search in two search engines and graphically illustrates the matching items. With a search for "therapy animals mental health" comparing Bing and Google results, this tool found 10 of the top 20 sites in common. That means that the combined top 20 has 30 unique items. To make matters more interesting, there was no overlap at all in the second group of 20 records, meaning that there are 40 unique websites in that group which give us a combined top 40 results that have 70 unique websites. Using a metasearch engine will return results that individual web search engines would miss alone. This may lead to information overload. How a metasearch engine chooses to display the results it finds becomes a very important part of its usability and a means to address the overload problem. You should try a few metasearch engines to find the one that works best for you.

Evaluating Websites

Because anyone can create a web page about anything and post it to the web without any editorial review, it is paramount that you evaluate the websites you are thinking of using in your research. Once again, we will use the three factors to evaluate websites.

Relevance

As we have seen before, relevance is easy to evaluate and the least important of the factors. If the website reflects your topic well, then it is relevant. If it does not embrace your topic, then move on. There are bound to be others that are a better match to your research question.

Purpose

Because there is no editorial control over the content of the Internet, you must examine closely the intent or purpose of the websites you are evaluating. There is a strong overlap between purpose and authority, here. We are asking why the page was created and that leads directly to the question of by whom. The three factors are interconnected and not distinct, separate factors. Look for how one affects another as you evaluate your websites.

Scope and Depth

Websites can offer very broad or very narrow coverage of broad or narrow topics. They can be very shallow or have tremendous depth. The websites you found for your research should already be focused on a subject. So we will be examining how much information on that subject they provide. Does it skim the surface of your topic and provide an overview, or does it dive deep and provide very long pages of information? Determine how relevant summary or extensive information is to your research need.

Style

Style, the choice of words and how they are used, is very important to determine the purpose of the website. Do the authors of the website use words to color and guide your thinking? For example, do they describe the group of people who do not support their position as "the opposition," "the small-minded opposition," or "the ill-informed opposition"? Do they continue on to describe the opposition's positions as "bogus," "bilious," "blatantly false," or "not supported by the evidence"? Do they talk about their own evidence as being "brilliant," "the best research," or do they just present it? If you get the impression that they are trying to convince you of their point but not through documented evidence, then there is a problem. You do not need to be sold facts. They speak for themselves. Point of view can be blatant or subtle. Be skeptical about what you are viewing until you can validate the information being presented.

Do not be influenced by the look of the website. The substance is more important than the style, and website authoring tools have made creating a good-looking website simple. You should expect a level of professionalism in the design of the website. More important than the look of the site is the organization of the information. It should be logical and easy to follow. The text should be free from spelling and grammar errors. The language should be neutral, and the intent should be to inform.

Validity

Validity is, again, the most important factor in the evaluation process and extremely important when examining web pages.

Timeliness

Publication dates are standard features of books, magazines, and journals. However, they may not appear on a web page. This is a problem. You need to know when the information was published or at least updated. Since there are so many potential websites to choose from, one without a publication date should come off your list.

There is not one spot where the date might be on the web page. You will need to look at the top of the page around the title and at the bottom of the page where there may be information about the site listed. Once you find a date, the previous guidelines apply. How old is the information, and does the information change quickly in this field? Some web pages will indicate the date they were published. This is typical of blogs, news sources, and web magazines. This is a hard publication date; that is, the whole thing was published at that time. Some will show a date the page was last modified. This is a soft date, parts were updated at this time, but the rest was not changed. It is hoped that this means the outdated information was changed. Others will show a date the page was copyrighted. This does not necessarily indicate that the information on the page was published or updated at that time. It may be a claim of ownership, instead. You will find dates like this on sites as diverse as Encyclopedia Britannica and the American Kennel Club. Because of these problems with dates, you need to confirm the information you find.

Authority

When evaluating websites, authority is very important and closely tied to purpose. Who wrote the page and what are their credentials is important to discover. Authority is a two-part question, who is the producer of the website, and who is the author of the web page? As with books and magazines, the reputation of the producer/publisher of the website should be examined. You may need to hunt around to find the name of the organization. It could be at the bottom of the page, in an About Us link, or part of the URL. Once you find who this is, then search for who they are and learn about the organization. Do they have a strong point of view or ideology that they are trying to promote through their website? If so, move on to the next web page you are considering. If they have a good reputation for presenting facts, then their web page is worth considering.

The author of the web page may be just as hard to find. If there is a publisher/producer, they may take credit for the content of the web page explicitly with a statement like, "Written by the staff of . . ." The credit could be implicit. In which case, there is no author listed, just the copyright statement. The credit or blame for the website is given to the corporate author, the organization, or entity that published the website.

Some websites with corporate authors also list the name of the author of the page you are evaluating. You will see this with web magazines and the Encyclopedia Britannica, for example. In this case, you can evaluate both the publishing organization and the author's credentials. Other websites only have an author, which shows that there is no larger, sponsoring organization. Look closely at authors' credentials. Hopefully, you can find this by clicking on their name, or examining their web page for the information or links to it. As before, you want the authors to have a background and degrees in the field. You want to confirm that they have expert knowledge, and if the style of the writing shows that they are not promoting a personal agenda, then you have only one more check to do.

There are web pages that have no author and no corporate attribution. Be very skeptical of a page like this. If they do not want to tell you who they are, then they are hiding something from you. It is best to discard that page from consideration and move on. If you still want to use it, then you must carefully judge its accuracy.

Accuracy

The less you know about the publisher and writer of the web page, the more important checking its accuracy becomes. That is not to say you can accept a web page as good because the publisher is reputable and the author has good credentials. That is a good start toward having a good web page. Accuracy involves confirming the information you have found in other resources. However, it is best not to use one web page to confirm the validity of the information on another web page, unless you have already confirmed the validity of that information with a number of other highly reputable and valid sources which are preferably not web pages.

Look for cited sources and bibliographies on the web pages you are evaluating. Check the dates and quality of the citations. Look for links to other sites, follow them, and evaluate those sites. Find out where the information on you web page originated. Keep in mind that the information could have originated with the author through research and authority. We mentioned the American Kennel Club before. If you want to know where they got their information on what a Fox Terrier or St. Bernard should look like, they are the creators and keepers of the standards for purebred dogs. You discovered that when you evaluated their authority.

With so many web pages to choose from, discard any from consideration if you have any suspicions about their accuracy. You should be able to find another page or another source where there is no question as to its accuracy.

Utilizing Web Sources

Finding the information you need on the web pages you found with your search statement is easy. You can read the whole page or you can search within the page to find a keyword and read from there. You can download and save web pages to any storage device. You can bookmark them using any number of programs and return to them at any time, and of course, you can copy and paste passage directly into other programs like your word processor. You can also take notes.

Web pages must be cited like any other source you quote, paraphrase, and summarize in your research project. Very few web pages offer a citation feature like commercial databases. You will need to copy down the important information for creating a citation or use citation management software both of which we will discuss in Chapter 9.

The Internet offers a wealth of information, and Internet search engines are very effective in finding that information, especially if you know how they work and what you can do to improve your search results. Finding the good items among the thousands of items retrieved is an essential skill to develop for both academic and personal information needs.

Vocabulary

advanced search commands	field searching
algorithm	implied Boolean AND
basic search	metasearch engines
bots	phrase searching
corporate author	profile
domain	relevancy ranking
facets	spiders

Questions for Reflection

What facets can be applied to Internet searches?

How is a metasearch like a federated search?

What is relevancy ranking, and how does it work?

How and why would you exclude a keyword from an Internet search?

Is it more important to evaluate web pages than journal articles? Why or why not?

How is validity affected by purpose when evaluating web pages?

Assignment

Open your research journal; take your research question from Chapter 2, and enter it in the Web Search and Item Evaluation Worksheet (Figures 7.5 and 7.6). Record the name of the search engine you are using, and the number of results your successful search statement found.

Find two good web pages from .com sites that directly address your research question. Copy the URL, publisher, author, and date information into the template if it is included. Evaluate each web page using our three factors and explain why each page is a quality resource. Pick the best web page and explain why it is the best choice for your research project.

Finally, look back on your previous work from Chapters 4 and 5 and compare and contrast it to your best resources from those chapters to your best web page. Pick the one item you think provides the information you need to best answer your research question.

Research Question:	
How has the reintroduction of wolves affected the ecosystem in Yellowstone National Park?	
Web Search Engine:	Bing
Search Statement and Number of Records Found:	
wolves ecosystem yellowstone site:.com	
1st Web Page	
Publisher and/or Author:	Science Daily
Title:	Wolves Are Rebalancing Yellowstone Ecosystem.
Date:	October 29, 2003
URL:	https://www.sciencedaily.com/ releases/2003/10/031029064909.htm
Evaluation of 1st web page	
Relevance:	
This site matches my research question very well.	
Purpose:	
Scope and Depth	
The web page has some length but not a lot, and is focused exclusively on my research question which is narrow.	
Style	
This is written to inform and presents the facts of the case. It is a news story.	
Validity:	
Timeliness	
Written in 2003, it is still up to date because wolves were reintroduced to Yellowstone National Park in 1995.	
Authority	
There is no author listed, the publisher is Science Daily, and they are an award-winning website that is the most popular science news site on the web. This gives it some credibility.	
Accuracy	
There are lots of quotes in the article, but there are no references. The information on this page is consistent with many other information sources it found, including research articles.	
Grade:	B
2nd Web Page	
Publisher and/or Author:	The Guardina, GrrlScientist

Figure 7.5: Web Search and Item Evaluation Worksheet Example

Title:	How Wolves Change Rivers
Date:	Monday March 3, 2014 10.23 EST
URL:	https://www.theguardian.com/science/ grrlscientist/2014/mar/03/how- wolves-change-rivers

Evaluation of 2ⁿᵈ Web Page

Relevance:
This is also a very relevant web page. It directly addresses my topic.

Purpose:
Scope and Depth
This is a short overview. It is narrowly focused, but has little depth. It is an introduction to a TED Talk.

Style
It is designed to inform. There are a couple of expressions that color the point-of-view but only a couple. It mostly presents facts.

Validity:
Timeliness
This is current as far as my topic goes. It features new information on how wolf predation has changed the rivers in Yellowstone.

Authority
The author's name is GrrlScientist. That's not good. But she is an evolutionary biologist and ornithologist who writes many articles for The Guardian which is a British national daily newspaper.

Accuracy
No sources are cited, but it is a news piece and an introduction to a full TED Talk which are very well regarded.

Grade:	B

Best Web Page and Why You Choose It:
Wolves Are Rebalancing Yellowstone Ecosystem.

This is my best web resource. It has more depth and addresses a few more aspects of my topic than the other web page. It is in a good source but does not have an author. Though it is listed as being from Oregon State University.

Title of Best Source from Chapter 4:
Wolves from *Environmental Encyclopedia*

Figure 7.5: (Continued)

Title of Best Source from Chapter 5:
Ecosystem Scale Declines in Elk Recruitment and Population Growth with Wolf Colonization: A Before-After-Control-Impact Approach.

Comparison and Contrast of Three Best Sources:
My best book source was a background source that had only brief information and an overview of my topic. This was better than my book source that was told from the point-of-view of a sheep rancher and had obvious bias. My background source is not as good as my web page because of the small amount of information. My web page did not have a lot of information either, but it was the most relevant source I found. It covered more impacts that wolves have had on the ecosystem than either my background source or my journal article. It has given me some ideas of what else to search for in more scholarly sources. My journal article is pretty relevant, though it focuses exclusively on the elk population. It was a big research study that included information from before the wolves were reintroduced and after they were introduced. This gives it very good information on the impact wolves have had on the elk population.

Best Overall Source:
My best information source is the scholarly journal article. It has the greatest depth of information, and is the most valid of the three sources because it has a lot of references, appeared in a peer-reviewed journal, and the authors all have degrees in the field. I do need to supplement this with other items because this does not have enough information to be the basis of my research.

Figure 7.5: (Continued)

Research Question:	
Web Search Engine:	
Search Statement and Number of Records Found:	
1st Web Page	
Publisher and/or Author:	
Title:	
Date:	
URL:	
Evaluation of 1st web page	
Relevance:	
Purpose: Scope and Depth / Style	
Validity: Timeliness / Authority / Accuracy	
Grade:	

2nd Web Page	
Publisher and/or Author:	
Title:	
Date:	
URL:	
Evaluation of 2nd Web Page	
Relevance:	
Purpose: Scope and Depth / Style	

Figure 7.6: Web Search and Item Evaluation Worksheet

Validity: Timeliness Authority Accuracy	
Grade:	
Best Web Page and Why You Choose It:	
Title of Best Source from Chapter 4:	
Title of Best Source from Chapter 5:	
Comparison and Contrast of Three Best Sources:	
Best Overall Source:	

Figure 7.6: (*Continued*)

CHAPTER 8

Evaluation of Your Research Process

In This Chapter

You will learn:

- How to evaluate search statements
- How to evaluate keywords
- How to choose an appropriate database
- How to evaluate and revise research questions

Why You Need to Evaluate Your Research Process

One of the reasons to evaluate your research process is to ensure that you did a good job. If your research is good, then it follows that the outcome of your research will be better. To ensure that your research process was good, you need to evaluate it. The three factors we used to evaluate information sources do not apply in this context. Instead, you need to hone your critical thinking skills and apply them to each aspect of the research process.

Critical thinking is a foundational life skill. It is a skill that you need to make good choices in your daily life from which presidential candidate will get your vote to which cereal to buy. You have already used critical thinking skills in evaluating information resources. Critical thinking is an active, intellectual process of logical thinking based on sound evidence. Critical thinking includes analyzing, comparing, contrasting, generalizing, investigating, experimenting, creating, conceptualizing, synthesizing, and evaluating information to achieve a goal, like solving a problem, planning a course of action, or conducting a research project that leads to a paper.

As you develop your critical thinking skills, you should be able to admit a lack of understanding or information and ask pertinent questions. This is how we grow and advance our knowledge. Critical thinking involves assessing arguments; examining beliefs, assumptions, and opinions; and weighing them against facts. It requires the suspension of judgment until all facts have been gathered and considered. It requires us to see the world in new ways when new facts are found. This assimilation of knowledge changes our thinking and leads to personal growth. Critical thinking necessitates an understanding of the importance of context and its influence on information, which we have already discussed. Critical thinking rejects information that is incorrect or irrelevant, and recognizes and corrects discrepancies. Critical thinking also means creative thinking when exploring and imagining alternatives, making connections between seemingly unrelated ideas, and drawing conclusions from a set of facts. Critical thinkers embrace the publication process to submit ideas and experiments for peer review, accept challenges and criticism to their work, listen carefully to others, and offer feedback and engage in reflective skepticism (Foundation for Critical Thinking 1997; McBrien and Brandt 1997; Petress 2004; Riddell 2007).

This long list may be intimidating, but it can be summed up as logical and rational questioning in pursuit of knowledge. Critical thinking is integral to evaluation. Evaluation is a process. It is not done once. It is a constant process. You are always evaluating your research and using your critical thinking skills.

Evaluating Your Research Process

We have introduced parts of evaluating the research process in previous chapters. We just did not call it evaluation. When we talked about modifying a search to find more or fewer articles, we were talking about evaluating your search. When we discussed changing your keywords to get better results or selecting a subject-specific database, we were discussing different parts of the research evaluation process.

Research is an iterative process. You need to try a search, evaluate it, and try it, again. Your first search reflects a number of decisions. You have your research question, you created a search statement using keywords derived from your question, and you picked a database to use for your search. You need to evaluate each of these parts of the research process and remember that these parts overlap, interconnect, and

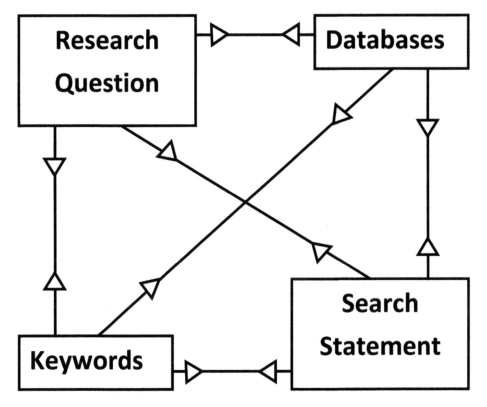

Figure 8.1: Research Process Evaluation and Effects of Changes

impact each other. A change to any one part may necessitate a change in any or all of the others. Figure 8.1 illustrates the four parts of evaluation in the research process.

Research Question

As far as your research question is concerned, your first set of results brings these questions. Do the results reflect on and address your research question? If not, why not? Is it the keywords, the search statement, the database, or does the problem lie with your research question?

In most cases, a research question needs to be refined after an initial search. You may find that your search returned too many, too few, or the wrong kind of results. Regardless of the outcome, the actions you need to take to correct the problem may be the same: Reevaluate your research question and revise your search statement, choose a different database, or just reformulate your search statement. This is illustrated in Figure 8.2.

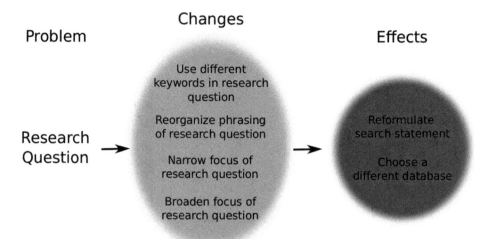

Figure 8.2: Research Question Evaluation: Changes and Effects

For example, if you found too few items, your research question could be too narrow. You need to restate your question in a broader manner, and maybe eliminate a concept from your search. A search statement with three ANDs is broader and will retrieve more than a search statement with four ANDs. If your research question seems good and your search statement seems accurate, then your keywords could be wrong, and you need to use a thesaurus to find alternatives, or check a relevant item from your results list and use keywords and subject terms you find there, or create a nested OR statement with synonyms for a concept, or change to a database that better matches the subject of your research question. Is your research question based on a discovery made a month earlier, then it may be too new to have much written about it? Any changes to your search statement may require you to change your research question. It could be just the terminology, or it could be the scope of your question.

Try restating your research question. This could help you find other words to search or lead to a different search statement. It may help you think about different ways to approach your topic or different aspects of your topic that you may want to examine. Make sure you are not searching for long phrases as these narrow your results greatly. Try searching each of your keywords individually to see if any of them are the problem. Finally, if nothing seems to be working, change your topic! Sometimes this is the best route to take. Your topic may simply be too obscure or too new to have much information and remember that the librarian is there to help you with all aspects of your research process.

Search Statement

The search statement is one of the easiest parts of the research process to change, and this makes it easy to evaluate. The search statement is your use of the Boolean operators, the phrase operator, and the other mechanics of the search. You should be using the database's advanced search screen as discussed in Chapter 4 and illustrated in Figure 4.4. It is a good visual representation of your search. Figure 8.3 illustrates some of the possible changes you can make to your search statement based on your initial search results (Figure 8.3).

If your search statement finds too many records, then the database is not the problem. Your search statement may have too few items that are being ANDed together, or you misused the OR operator which broadened your search in an unexpected way. If you used an OR statement in your search, make sure that OR is being used to group together synonyms, and that the group of synonyms is being ANDed to another keyword or concept. Applying facets is a quick way to reduce the number of items retrieved by a search, and they will help you get the types of materials you need, for instance, full-text scholarly journal articles.

Keywords

Keywords have a great impact on your search results. The wrong keyword will not describe your topic well and return incomplete or even inaccurate results. The following example illustrates why you need to evaluate your keywords. You search for:

- airfoils AND turbines AND efficiency

This search finds a good number of journal articles, 75. You also notice that there are similar keywords being used in the subject field. Your next search is for:

- aerofoils AND turbines AND efficiency

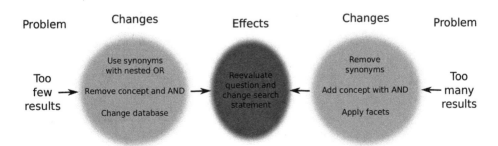

Figure 8.3: Search Statement Evaluation: Changes and Effects

This search returns fewer articles overall and fewer journal articles at 55. Your keyword seems to be better than the subject term. Then again, you noticed one other subject term and you try that in your next search:

- aerodynamics AND turbines AND efficiency

This search returns more than 280 journal articles. The keyword "aerodynamics" best represents your topic. It has high relevance. It also has high retrieval and you will want to add another concept to your search to narrow its focus and make a corresponding change to your research question or apply facets to reduce the overall number of items retrieved. Figure 8.4 illustrates these options.

Choosing the right keywords to search is the difference between a successful search and a failed one. Finding the right keywords can involve trial and error and a little digging. Execute your search statement. Examine your results for relevant records. Examine relevant records for your keywords. Pay close attention to the subject terms of those records. Did one or more of your keywords show up here? If not, what terms were used? Do these terms describe your topic? If so, use these subject terms to modify your search.

Database Selection

Which database you choose to search will have a big impact on your search results. You would not search for Van Gogh in Agricola, a database that covers all aspects of agriculture, but you *would* search for Van Gogh in Art Full Text.

As we mentioned before, you can always start your search in a general database like Academic Search Premier, which covers all subject

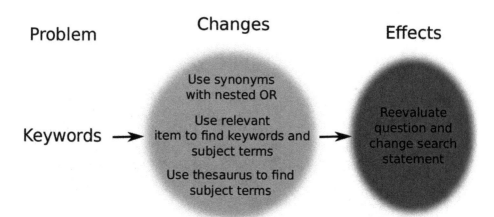

Figure 8.4: Keyword Evaluation: Changes and Effects

areas. Because it is a general database, it has breadth, but not as much depth as a subject-specific database. A general database will have many items about Van Gogh and also many items about invasive species. However, subject-specific databases like Art Full Text and Agricola will contain many more records about Shakespeare and many more focused records about invasive species, respectively. While more information may be confusing, a large result set for one keyword is good. It means that you have more records to combine with your other key concepts and that leads to finding the specific records that reflect your research question without encountering a search that results in zero items. For example, this search

- "van gogh" AND brushwork

found zero records in a general database. That same search in Art Full Text found seven records. This search

- "invasive species" AND "climate change" AND ecosystems

found more than 300 journal articles in our general database, while the same search found 112 journal articles in Agricola. The difference is that the articles in Agricola are further limited to agriculture by the scope of the contents of the database. It is like having a fourth search term. In fact, adding the fourth term "agriculture" to the search in the general database finds only 34 journal articles. Depending on your topic, your best choice may be a subject-specific database because it will retrieve more and more relevant records (Figure 8.5).

If you checked your search statement and it looks good, and if you tried your keywords and they seem appropriate, but your search is finding too few records or no records, then the problem lies with the

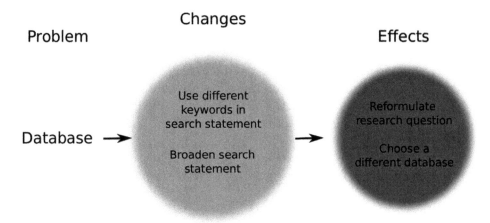

Figure 8.5: Database Evaluation: Changes and Effects

database you are searching. Try different keywords. Try broadening your search statement. If that does not improve your results, move from a general to a subject-specific database. Switch from one subject-specific database to another, or if your library has it, try federated searching to find relevant records and the databases that contain them.

Vocabulary

critical thinking

database selection

evaluation of the research process

keywords

research process

research question

search statement

Questions for Reflection

Why is it important to evaluate your research process?

How do you determine if there is a problem with your search statement or keywords?

What impact does your choice of database have on your research process?

How do you determine if your research question is good or bad?

Assignment

Open your research journal, take your research question and search statement from your last assignment, and rerun it in a general database. Examine and evaluate the first 20 search results for retrieval, relevance, and quality of records found. Next, run the same search statement in an appropriate subject database, and perform the same evaluation. If your library does not have subject-specific databases, then write a search statement on a topic in education or library science, and execute it in your library's general database. Then go to ERIC (http://eric.ed.gov), a free government database created by the Institute of Education Sciences that covers all aspects of education and many aspects of library science, and rerun your new search (Figures 8.6 and 8.7).

Finally, compare the first 20 search results from the general and subject-specific databases. Choose the database that provides the best answer to your research question and explain why you made that choice.

Research Question: Do school uniforms have any impact on student academic achievement?	
Search Statement: school uniforms AND academic achievement	
General Database Name:	Academic Search Premier
Number of Records Found:	23
Evaluation of Search Results: Eight of the items found in the search were from popular magazines and 15 are from journals. That's about 1/3 from popular sources. I thought I would find more items than this. So the retrieval seems low. A few of the items were not even about my topic. Many other items did not really focus on academic achievement, but mentioned it. So even with a good number of peer-reviewed items, the search results were disappointing.	
Grade for Search Results:	C
Subject Specific Database:	ERIC
Number of Records Found:	195
Evaluation of Search Results: Only 56 of the items were journal articles, but most of the rest were research reports, and none were from popular sources. There were a lot more items retrieved, and there were more that were not relevant. The items all seem scholarly and should be generally good.	
Grade for Search Results:	C
Best Database:	ERIC
Reasons for Choosing it: Even though so many of the items weren't relevant to my research question, I had a larger result set that I could add a third term to and narrow the results to get better results. Also, there were a bunch of facets I could apply to help focus the results on my topic. Then I would have more and better results than I found in Academic Search Premier.	

Figure 8.6: Subject-Specific Database Evaluation Worksheet Example

Research Question:	
Search Statement:	
General Database Name:	
Number of Records Found:	
Evaluation of Search Results:	
Grade for Search Results:	
Subject-Specific Database:	
Number of Records Found:	
Evaluation of Search Results:	
Grade for Search Results:	
Best Database:	
Reasons for Choosing it:	

Figure 8.7: Subject-Specific Database Evaluation Worksheet

CHAPTER 9

Managing Information

In This Chapter

You will learn:

- What your role is in the research community
- What a citation is and the citation styles available
- What citation managers are and how to use them
- How to create citations and bibliographies in your research papers

Your Role in the Research Community

Research is not done in isolation. This simple statement has broad implications. It means that we work within a community of scholars who are concerned with the same issues we are. It means that we ask questions and follow a process like the scientific method, the formulation and testing of hypotheses through observation and experimentation, to perform research and explore answers within our community. It means we participate in scholarly communication by reading journal articles, performing research, sharing our results, and talking to other scholars. It means we are literate, able to function within, and knowledgeable about the research process, the publication process, and the social context of the field within which we operate. It means we know how to examine the literature with a critical eye and an understanding of its meaning.

Isaac Newton said, "If I have seen further it is by standing on the shoulders of giants" ("Isaac Newton" 2016). Newton was saying that progress is made by building on previous knowledge and that we cannot achieve new discoveries alone. You may not stand as tall as Newton, but you are standing on giants' shoulders, as well.

Asking questions and exploring for answers through original or secondary research make you part of the scholarly community. Certain expectations come with your entry. You are expected to conduct yourself ethically. That includes respecting the ideas of others and not taking credit for them, and conducting your research in a responsible and legal manner. The data you collect should not be manipulated and your analysis of it valid. Good research, your research, adds to the conversation that takes place within the community and furthers our base of knowledge. You are helping to build a taller giant.

Citations

When you quote, paraphrase, or summarize an information source in your research paper, you need to attribute that information to its source. You do this with a citation. A citation has two parts. The first is the in-text citation, which gives very brief information like the author's last name, year of publication, and page number or it may simply be a number. This is then associated with an alphabetical bibliography or numbered notes which are the second part of the citation that includes the full bibliographic information. What constitutes the full bibliographic information depends on the type of information source you are citing and the citation style you are using. It includes, but is not limited to, the names of the authors, title of the piece, and publication information.

There are four components included in a basic book citation as shown in Figure 9.1. These components can be ordered in different

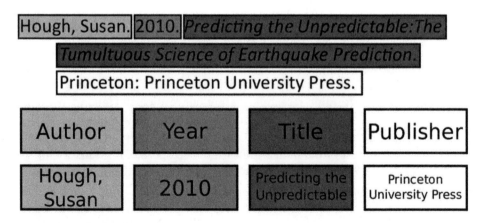

Figure 9.1: Components of a Book Citation

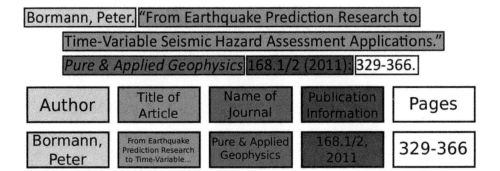

Figure 9.2: Components of a Journal Citation

ways, and the content of each component follows a set of rules for formatting the information.

The typical components of a journal citation include five components as illustrated in Figure 9.2. Again, the order of the components varies, and the context follows specific formatting rules.

Citation Styles

What determines the order of the elements and the formatting of their content is the citation style being used. There are literally thousands of different citation styles that are specific to different disciplines and journals. Three of the more popular citation styles are APA developed by the American Psychological Association and used in psychology, MLA from the Modern Language Association and used in English, and Chicago which was developed at the University of Chicago and used in history. Your instructor should assign a citation style for you to use. This style will determine how both your in-text citation and bibliography should look. Figures 9.3 and 9.4 show a book and a journal article in each of the three formats mentioned earlier.

You will need to look closely to see the minor differences between them.

There is not much sense to the difference in citations styles. They were created by different organizations to serve the unique needs of their fields or by the journal to serve their needs. You will be asked to write papers in multiple styles throughout your scholastic careers. All of these styles with their minor differences lead to confusion and unnecessary complication when you have to cite your sources. Keep the components of a citation in mind and find help when you have questions.

Style	In-Text Citation	Bibliography
APA	*Without author in signal phrase:* One source concludes, ". . ." (Hough, 2010, p. 21). *With author in signal phrase:* In her book, Hough (2010) states, ". . ." (p. 21).	Hough, S. (2010). *Predicting the unpredictable: The tumultuous science of earthquake prediction.* Princeton, NJ: Princeton University Press.
Chicago	*Without author in signal phrase:* One source concludes, ". . ." (Hough, 2010 21). *With signal phrase:* In her book, Hough (2010) states, ". . ." (21).	Hough, Susan. 2010. *Predicting the Unpredictable: The Tumultuous Science of Earthquake Prediction.* Princeton: Princeton University Press.
MLA	*Without author in signal phrase:* One source concludes, ". . ." (Hough 21). *With signal phrase:* In her book, Hough states, ". . ." (21).	Hough, Susan. *Predicting the Unpredictable: The Tumultuous Science of Earthquake Prediction.* Princeton: Princeton UP, 2010. Print.

Figure 9.3: Book Citation in Three Formats

Style	In-Text Citation	Bibliography
APA	*Without author in signal phrase:* One source concludes, ". . ." (Bormann, 2011, p. 329). *With author in signal phrase:* In the article by Bormann (2011), he states, ". . ." (p. 21).	Bormann, P. (2011). From earthquake prediction research to time-variable seismic hazard assessment applications. *Pure & Applied Geophysics, 168*(1/2), 329–366. doi:10.1007/ s00024-010-0114-0
Chicago	*Without author in signal phrase:* One source concludes, ". . ." (Bormann 2011, 329). *With author in signal phrase:* In the article by Bormann (2011), he states, ". . ." (21).	Bormann, Peter. 2011. "From Earthquake Prediction Research to Time-Variable Seismic Hazard Assessment Applications." *Pure & Applied Geophysics* 168 (1/2) (January): 329–366. doi:10.1007/s00024-010-0114-0.

Figure 9.4: Journal Citation in Three Formats

| MLA | *Without author in signal phrase:*
One source concludes, ". . ."
(Bormann 329).

With author in signal phrase:
In the article by Bormann, he
states, ". . ." (21). | Bormann, Peter. "From Earthquake Pre-
diction Research to Time-Variable
Seismic Hazard Assessment Applica-
tions." *Pure & Applied Geophysics*
168.1/2 (2011): 329–366. |

Figure 9.4: (*Continued*)

Citation Help

There are many ways to get help with citing sources. There are books from the creators of the format like *MLA Handbook*, *Publication Manual*, and *Chicago Manual of Style* for MLA, APA, and Chicago, respectively. Then there are books like *A Pocket Style Manual* that cover the three big formats mentioned earlier in one short book. All of these books can be found in your library's collections. Websites like Purdue OWL (https://owl.english.purdue.edu/owl/) cover the major formats and make it easy to find examples that relate to your specific situation, as in multiple authors, edited works, translations, and works with no authors. Any of these resources will help you with many examples of how to cite books, journals, movies, interviews, websites, and other materials.

Citation Managers

Another route to take is a citation manager. Not only will they help you create your citations in multiple formats, but they will also enable you to keep track of your research. Managing all the information you find is an important aspect of the research process. A good management system will allow you to easily find an item within it that you previously found in a search. It will allow you to read, highlight, and take notes on the materials you found. It will allow you to move items around to organize them in folders and subfolders that make sense to you and add your own keywords to items. Of course, they will also help you create an in-text citation and bibliography.

Database Citation Managers

Most commercial databases generate a bibliographic citation in a few of the major formats. This is an important fact because the information displayed in a database results list or in an individual record is *not* a citation. You need to use the citation generator to get a citation. You can generate a citation for an individually displayed record or for a list of marked items.

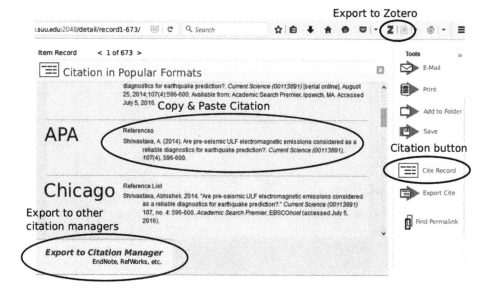

Figure 9.5: Database Citation Generator

Figure 9.5 shows the citation button in the database. Once this is clicked, the various citation formats are displayed in a scrolling list. You can copy and paste any of the displayed styles into your word processor. However, you may need to format the citation with a hanging indention and double spacing. You can directly export the citation to a number of citation managers listed at the bottom of the image or you can click on the article icon next to the "Z" at the top of the image to import the citation into Zotero.

In addition, most databases offer a free account that has many features of a citation manager. After registering for an account, you will be able to create folders and save the records you found into them. Without an account, all your research for that session disappears when you log out. With an account, you can create a folder called Research Paper and save the items that you are considering using in your paper. Then as you write, you can create a folder called Items Used in Paper and move the records of the items you use into that folder. When you are done, you can select all the records in your Items Used in Paper folder and have the database generate a bibliography for you. This is a nice feature.

Other features you can access with an account are the ability to save your search statements. This is handy as it allows you to refer back to the search that found your best results. You can also rerun the search to see if any new information has been added to the database that matches your search. You can even set up your search to run automatically at given intervals for just that purpose. This is called a search alert. One last feature is the journal alert. If you read or browse the same magazines and journals every time a new issue comes out, a journal alert will help by sending you the table of contents for each new issue. If the database contains the full text, then you also receive a link to the articles in the magazines and journals on your list of journal alerts whether your tastes run toward *Opera News* or toward *Rolling Stone*. The citation manager features provided in databases are not robust, and you may want to use something else for these features, but the other features are definitely worth exploring.

Software Citation Managers

Websites like EasyBib (http://www.easybib.com/cite/view) will help you produce good citations and even have some shortcuts for finding books and other materials. EasyBib also offers a version that is available for your school to purchase, and it offers more management features. KnightCite (http://www.calvin.edu/library/knightcite/) and Noodle Tools Express (http://www.noodletools.com/noodlebib/express.php) will both help you produce a good citation, but you must enter all the information manually. Word processors have built-in features to help you create both your in-text cite and your bibliography, but they also require you to input all of your citation information first.

Commercial software like EndNote (http://endnote.com/) and Ref-Works (https://refworks.proquest.com/), along with freeware programs like Zotero (https://www.zotero.org/) and Mendeley (https://www.mendeley.com/), are true citation managers which not only help you generate your entire bibliography but also help you track and organize all of your information sources, create multiple notes for any item, and add your own keywords to imported subject headings. Unlike their database counterparts, these programs can change the case of titles to match the format required by the specified styles. They also have the benefit of "cite while you write" add-ins for word processing programs like Word and Writer from LibreOffice that make it easy to properly insert your in-text citation, then generate your bibliography from the in-text citations you used.

Additionally, these programs import the full bibliographic information from many databases. They even do a good job of finding and importing citation information from web pages. This saves you the typing of the bibliographic information and prevents the errors that may occur from that. You can create your own citations for information that you did not find by using a web browser or for an item for which the program cannot create a citation.

These tools are time savers and are very useful. However, they do make mistakes. Databases cannot change the case of fields when creating a citation for a record. So if the record has the title in all capital letters, your citation ends up with an all-capital title that is wrong in all citation styles. It is important that you know what citations should look like for the style you need to use in order to avoid these kinds of mistakes. Be sure to consult official publications or style guides in print or on the web to make sure you understand how your citations should look.

Inserting Citations and Bibliographies into Research Papers

Cite-while-you-write and bibliography generation is a great feature of citation managers. In Figure 9.6, the add-in for Zotero has been added to LibreOffice Writer. The add-in consists of the first seven icons on the second row of icons. The first icon inserts an in-text

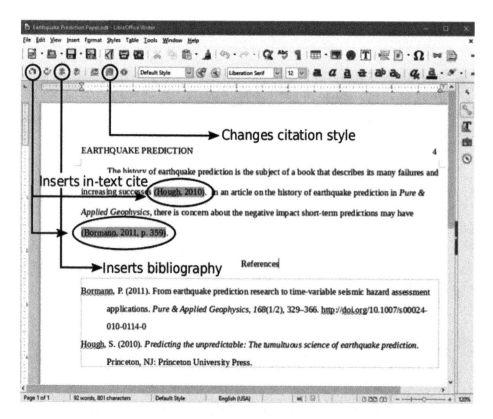

Figure 9.6: In-Text Citations and Bibliography with Zotero

citation at the cursor. After clicking on the icon, you get a list of all your records that you have saved. You can pick the item from the list or search for it. If your item is in a folder, selecting that folder will make it the default folder for the rest of your writing session. Once you pick an item, you can include the page number where the quote was found. The first in-text citation was a summary of the book and therefore does not need a page number. The second in-text citation paraphrases what the author said, for example, on page 359 of the journal.

The third Zotero icon inserts a bibliography based on your in-text citations into your paper at the cursor. The citation style for this example is APA. The APA style requires a double-spaced bibliography, and Zotero produces that automatically. To change the style to any other, click on the sixth icon, which looks like a gear and pick the style you want from the list presented. You will see both the in-text citations and bibliography change to match the formatting requirements of the selected citation style.

As a point of information, there were three errors in the bibliography that had to be fixed, one error in the first entry and two in the second. All the errors were minor, but citation styles are unforgiving. If you do not catch the errors, you need to have a forgiving instructor.

Vocabulary

bibliography

book citation

citation

citation managers

citation styles

cite-while-you-write

full bibliographic information

in-text citation

journal alerts

journal citation

notes

paraphrase

quote

scholarly communication

scientific method

search alerts

summarize

Questions for Reflection

Why are there so many different citation styles?

What advantages does a database-based citation manager have over a true citation manager?

What advantages does a true citation manager offer that a database-based citation manager does not?

What are the differences between citation styles?

Assignment

Open your research journal, and rerun your search in a database of your choice for a journal article on your topic. From the results list, copy and paste the citation information into the Citation Worksheet (Figures 9.7 and 9.8). Identify the parts of the citation and copy and paste them into the appropriate spaces.

Next, use the database's citation generator to create a citation for the journal article in both the APA and MLA styles. Copy these citations into the appropriate boxes. Use a citation manager to generate an APA and MLA citation for the same journal article. Your school may have licensed a product for you to use. If so, use that citation manager. If you are not sure if your school has a citation manager, ask your librarian. If your school does not have a citation manager, use Zotero or Mendeley which are both free to generate your citations.

Create a corrected, perfect, citation in both APA and MLA formats. You may need to consult a book for the styles or a web page to make sure you get each citation exactly correct.

Finally, explain whether the database or the citation manager generated the most accurate citations, what mistakes were made, and the magnitude of those mistakes. Explain your choice. Then pick the citation style you like best and explain your reasons for that choice.

Find a Journal Article	
Database Used:	Academic Search Premier
Citation Manager Used:	Zotero
Copy from Results List:	Are pre-seismic ULF electromagnetic emissions considered as a reliable diagnostics for earthquake prediction? By: Shrivastava, Abhishek. Current Science (00113891). 8/25/2014, Vol. 107 Issue 4, p596–600. 5p.

Figure 9.7: Citation Worksheet Example

	Subjects: EARTHQUAKE prediction; EARTH-QUAKE magnitude; SEISMIC event location; RELIABILITY (Engineering); ELECTROMAG-NETIC fields

Components of the Journal Citation	
Author(s):	Shrivastava, Abhishek
Title of Article:	Are pre-seismic ULF electromagnetic emissions considered as a reliable diagnostics for earthquake prediction?
Name of Journal:	Current Science
Publication Information:	8/25/2014, Vol. 107 Issue 4
Pages:	p596–600

Database Generated APA Cite:	Shrivastava, A. (2014). Are pre-seismic ULF electromagnetic emissions considered as a reliable diagnostics for earthquake prediction?. Current Science (00113891), 107(4), 596–600.
Citation Manager APA Cite:	Shrivastava, A. (2014). Are pre-seismic ULF electromagnetic emissions considered as a reliable diagnostics for earthquake prediction? Current Science (00113891), 107(4), 596–600.
Corrected APA Citation:	Shrivastava, A. (2014). Are pre-seismic ULF electromagnetic emissions considered as a reliable diagnostics for earthquake prediction? Current Science, 107(4), 596–600.

Database Generated MLA Cite:	Shrivastava, Abhishek. "Are Pre-Seismic ULF Electromagnetic Emissions Considered As A Reliable Diagnostics For Earthquake Prediction?." Current Science (00113891) 107.4 (2014): 596–600. Academic Search Premier. Web. 5 July 2016.
Citation Manager MLA Cite:	Shrivastava, Abhishek. "Are Pre-Seismic ULF Electromagnetic Emissions Considered as a Reliable Diagnostics for Earthquake Prediction?" Current Science (00113891) 107.4 (2014): 596–600. Print.

Figure 9.7: (*Continued*)

Corrected MLA Citation:	Shrivastava, Abhishek. "Are Pre-Seismic ULF Electromagnetic Emissions Considered as a Reliable Diagnostics for Earthquake Prediction?" *Current Science* 107.4 (2014): 596–600. Print.
Which Service Generated the Best Citation and Why?	Zotero generated the best citations. The database had trouble with question marks and added a period following them. That's wrong. The databases also did not double space automatically like Zotero did. Both of these styles require double spacing. The database added additional information about where and when the record was found in its MLA citation. This is not necessary. Zotero did make a mistake by including that number following the name of the journal, but that was all it got wrong.
Which Citation Style do You Prefer and Why?	Though I do not like the DOI part of the APA style, my article did not have a DOI. So that was nice. Otherwise, I think APA is a little easier with sentence case for the article title. It is also a little easier to see the year that an article was published since it follows after the author, and that makes it easier to evaluate the sources.

Figure 9.7: (*Continued*)

Find a Journal Article	
Database Used:	
Citation Manager Used:	
Copy from Results List:	
Components of the Journal Citation	
Author(s):	
Title of Article:	
Name of Journal:	
Publication Information:	
Pages:	
Database Generated APA Cite:	
Citation Manager APA Cite:	
Corrected APA Citation:	
Database Generated MLA Cite:	
Citation Manager MLA Cite:	
Corrected MLA Citation:	
Which Service Generated the Best Citation and Why?	
Which Citation Style Do You Prefer and Why?	

Figure 9.8: Citation Worksheet

CHAPTER 10

Ethical Use of Information

In This Chapter

You will learn:

- How to use and synthesize information
- How to quote, paraphrase, and summarize from an information source
- The importance of citing sources and the consequences of plagiarism
- What intellectual property, copyright, and fair use are

Using Information

There are a right way, a wrong way, and a very wrong way to use information in your research projects. We use information all the time throughout our lives to make the best decisions we can at the time. We use information to make personal decisions like which diet is best for our health and professional decisions based on the feedback from a focus group about which advertising campaign will work best for our product. No matter the information need, we know we need good information to make the best decisions. We have learned how to find and evaluate information to ensure we have quality information sources. However, when it comes to research projects, we need to do one more thing. We need to use the information ethically.

The ethical use of information is one of the most important concepts in information literacy. It is a part of the definition of information literacy. If you cannot use information in an ethical manner, you are not information literate. It is a pillar of information literacy, and it has important ramifications.

Quoting, Paraphrasing, and Summarizing Information

The right way to use information in a research project is to quote, paraphrase, and summarize it, then attribute the information to its creator. You want to use good information from reputable sources to support your arguments and ultimately support your hypothesis. The first method for including information from others in your paper is to directly quote it. Use a quotation only when the exact wording from the original sources is impactful and important to use. In Figure 10.1, it was thought that quoting the authors gave an obvious statement some authority.

The first part of the first sentence in the figure is called a signal phrase. A signal phrase sets up the quote, paraphrase, or summary that follows with an introduction to whom or what you are using in your paper. You should not allow the material you use from others to stand alone. It needs to be interpreted and integrated into your work. Explain what the quote means or how the paraphrase supports the point you are making in that paragraph.

If you do not need to use the exacting wording from your information source, then you should paraphrase. Paraphrasing is restating the author's point in your own words, perhaps to shorten the passage from the original. Paraphrasing also shows an understanding of the author's work and is an important part of synthesizing information. You cannot write a good paraphrase unless you gained some understanding of the author's intent. Paraphrasing someone else's words is not easy. You cannot use the original author's language, word choices, and phrases. If you find that you cannot restate without using phrases from the original work, then you are better off using a quotation.

In Figure 10.2, a fact from the article is paraphrased. There is no need to quote this information. The fact is direct and to the point.

In a research article on why students resort to unethical practices, the authors point out that "College students are interested in achieving their academic goals. That said, students may sometimes try to attain their goals dishonestly" (Griffin, Bolkan, and Goodboy 9).

Figure 10.1: Quoting from an Article

For their research, Griffin, Bolkan, and Goodboy asked college students why they cheat. More than 82% of students were motivated to cheat in order to achieve a higher grade (9).

Figure 10.2: Paraphrasing from an Article

One study reported that students use deception in the classroom for two major reason, to get better grades and to manage the impression others have of them, and since students think their deception succeeds almost 92% of the time, whether minor or major, they are unlikely to change their behavior unless the instructor creates an atmosphere of trust and allows for mistakes to be made in a supportive environment (Griffin, Bolkan, and Goodboy).

Figure 10.3: Summary of an Article

Finally, you may choose to summarize an article, a book chapter, or a book in your research project. A summary is a short overview of the work written in your own words and cover the main ideas of the work. Summarizing is different from paraphrasing. Paraphrasing should represent an idea or a passage from the work, while a summary represents the whole work.

Figure 10.3 shows a summary of the same research article we have quoted from and paraphrased (Griffin, Bolkan, and Goodboy 2015). It covers the major findings of the article and even the authors' suggestions for decreasing student deception. Summaries are harder to incorporate into a research project for the obvious reason that you need to use all the work's major points to support your own thinking. The summary in the figure can be used to show why students use deception and the importance of doing something about it whether that be using a plagiarism detection service to increase the odds of getting caught or creating a classroom environment that allows students to explore opinions and ideas without fear of failure.

Intellectual Property and Copyright

Intellectual property is the product of your research, hard work, and imagination. Intellectual property is "creations of the mind" (World Intellectual Property Organization 2016). Those creations may lead to a patent for a product or invention, a trademark for a symbol or sign used to represent a product or service, or a copyrighted work. The creators of intellectual property are granted legal rights and protections for the use of their creations.

Information literacy is primarily concerned with the use of copyrighted materials because it is these materials you will use in your research and in your daily life. Copyright is a legal form of protection provided to the authors of "original works of authorship," which includes literary, dramatic, musical, artistic, film, dance, and other creative/intellectual works (U.S. Copyright Office 2012, 3). You have the right to make money from your work, and you can license or sell your work to others to display, perform, or create derivative works like turning your novel into a movie.

You do not have to apply for copyright. It is automatic. If you create a web page, it is copyrighted from the moment it is "fixed in a copy" the first time (U.S. Copyright Office 2012, 3). The concept of "copy" is broad and fits with all the possible formats mentioned earlier. Copyright is very easily obtained, and the rights it gives the creator are substantial. You own the copyright to your term papers and whatever else you create unless you sign a statement giving up those rights.

Terms of use agreements may take away your copyright protections. Terms of use agreements are legally binding contracts that spell out what you agree to do in order to use a website, service, or software. For example, you may sign up for an account on a website that allows you to create posts in response to articles published there. In order to create your account, you have to agree to the terms of use which may state that the website has the right to distribute, copy, and create derivative works from your posts without compensating you. In other words, you gave up your copyright to your creative work.

Fair Use

Another very important limit to a creator's copyright protection is called fair use. Fair use is an essential idea in our society as it allows a way in which the creator's work can be used without the need to obtain permission or compensate them. Fair use grants everyone limited rights to use copyrighted works. This includes using copyrighted works for the purpose of scholarship or research.

There are four factors listed in the law to consider when determining if your use of copyrighted materials is fair (U.S. Copyright Office 2016). The first is the nature of the use you plan to put the material to. Using copyrighted works for educational purposes favors fair use, but using them for commercial purposes favors the copyright holder. Next is the nature of the document you plan to use. If the document is largely factual, it favors fair use, because facts and ideas cannot be copyrighted, but an author's expression of those facts, how the author states them, can. The third factor is the amount of the work you intend to use. The more you use, the less fair that use is to the copyright holder. The fourth factor is how your use of the copyrighted work impacts its market value. For example, if you make a copy of a song and distribute it to 100 of your friends, you have denied the artist, the copyright holder, 100 potentials sales and the royalties from those sales. Not only you have violated copyright, but you have also broken the law.

If you are not sure if the use you plan for a copyrighted work is legal under the fair use doctrine, check with your librarian. They can offer you guidance, though not a legal opinion. If you are still unsure, then contact the copyright holder and ask for permission. Another option is to change your use to one that is fairer in nature.

Many works are in the public domain. Works that are in the public domain are not protected by copyright, and fair use does not apply. These works are free to be used as you see fit. This includes everything published before 1923 (Fishman 2008, 5). Another category of information that is free of copyright is information produced by the government. Government documents are produced by all agencies of the government, and by law cannot be copyrighted (USA.Gov 2016). The U.S. government collects and publishes large amounts of statistical information which as facts are not subject to copyright in any event. Authors may choose to place their works in the public domain or use Creative Commons Licenses that allows for varying degrees of protection and use, including a simple attribution license that allows use for any purpose as long as the creator is given credit (Creative Commons 2016). Giving credit is important for all items used in your research whether they are copyrighted, in the public domain, or have a Creative Commons license and that means quoting accurately and citing appropriately. If you do not do this, you have plagiarized.

Plagiarism

Plagiarism is claiming someone else's ideas as your own. It is a lie you tell the audience of your work. You let them believe that you are the creator of an idea. It is theft of intellectual property. Even if you forget to cite a source in your research paper, you have committed plagiarism though that was not your intent. However, it is not illegal. You will not go to jail for plagiarism. You will not be fined for plagiarizing someone else's work.

Plagiarism does have consequences. These consequences vary by the severity of the infraction and your school's policies. You may receive a light punishment like receiving a failing grade on the assignment, or your punishment might be more severe. You may receive a failing grade for the class, be placed on academic probation, or even be dismissed from school. There are real-world consequences for plagiarism, as well. Recently, a senator from Montana was found to have plagiarized in his master's thesis. His degree was revoked, and he withdrew from his campaign for reelection (Martin 2014).

In the past, instructors relied on their experience and knowledge of students' previous work to detect plagiarism. Now they use services like Turnitin (http://turnitin.com) which make it easy to detect plagiarism. Turnitin is a very large service that compares your electronic document to all the other papers submitted from your class, your school, other schools around the world, and sites across the web to find matches to the wording in your document. Turnitin shows the instructor the parts of your report that match other documents and those other documents, and what percentage of your paper matches other papers. The instructor checks those matches, makes a decision about whether you plagiarized, and decides what consequences you will face.

Synthesizing Information

Synthesis of information is bringing new ideas into your worldview, your personal information context, and combining it with what you know to form a new, more complex understanding. Synthesis is a learning process. Figure 10.4 illustrates part 2 of the Pathways Information Seeking Model. Part 1 ended with your initial discovery of information and what you do with it. You can deny the veracity of the information, use it to confirm your existing knowledge, or accept that it is new information.

Part 2 of the model picks up at a decision point. You have to decide what you are going to do with the information from your initial discovery. It can decrease your motivation and interest in the subject. It can lead to no change in your motivation. Perhaps you already had a high interest or no interest, and your first brush with the information did nothing to change that. It can increase your motivation and interest to learn about the subject.

A low level of interest leads to a low level of learning. In this case, we call it surface learning. This is the information you cannot help but learn by doing a research project on a topic. It is minimal learning that will not stick, perhaps because you do not want it to last. Next is strategic learning, which is learning enough to achieve a goal of earning a B or even an A in class, for example. Learning about the topic is

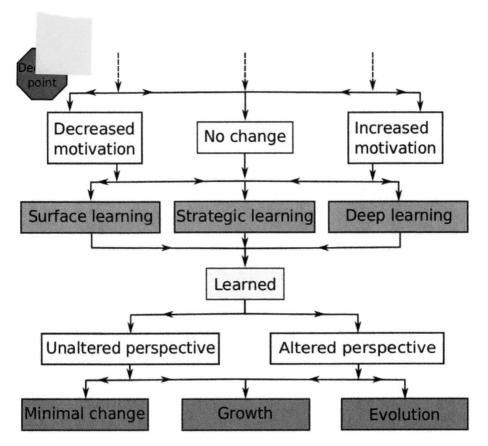

Figure 10.4: Pathways Information Seeking Model—Part 2

secondary to earning the desired grade. Then there is deep learning. This usually comes from a high interest in the topic. Learning the subject is important to you.

The next step on the chart is what you learned. This is formally assessed by your instructor and takes the form of a grade. However, this needs to be informally evaluated by you. What did you learn about the process and the subject matter? This is where you determine if you did answer your information need. If you denied the information you found and engaged in surface learning, then there is little change in perspective and little growth.

Learning can alter your perspective. An altered perspective is growth. You are becoming smarter, wiser, and more knowledgeable. An altered perspective may also lead to a major change in who you are and what you understand. It can lead to your evolution as a person. This is a more fundamental change to who you are and what your interests are. This may be the change that leads you to your career.

Growth and evolution are signs of synthesis. You integrated new information into your information environment. This means you have developed a level of understanding of your topic, and you can express that understanding in your own words. It also means that you are formulating your own ideas based on your new learning and existing knowledge. This is what you express in your research project, your synthesis of ideas, and the new knowledge you have developed.

Vocabulary

copyright	quoting
Creative Commons	signal phrase
deep learning	strategic learning
ethical use of information	summarizing
fair use	surface learning
intellectual property	synthesis
paraphrasing	terms of use
plagiarism	Turnitin
public domain	using information

Questions for Reflection

What does it mean to use information ethically?

What is fair use?

How do you integrate a quote into your research project?

Is plagiarism illegal, and what are the consequences of plagiarizing?

What does it mean to synthesize information?

Assignment

Open your research journal and find two good scholarly articles on your topic. Decide which citation style you will use for this assignment from APA, Chicago, and MLA. Read the articles and find an important quote from each article (Figures 10.5 and 10.6).

Use a signal phrase and incorporate that quote into a sentence that you would use in a research paper. Include the in-text citation. The quote from your first article should not include the authors' names in your signal phrase.

Next following the guidelines from above, create a sentence where you paraphrase that same quotation.

Finally using those same guidelines, summarize the article.

Repeat the process with your second article, but this time, use the authors' names in the signal phrases.

Lastly, generate a bibliography in your selected format for the two items making sure that each citation is correct.

Citation Style:	APA
1st Article, without author in signal phrase	
Quotation:	In a research article from 2012, it was found that "students do not acquire IL skills on their own even when they are given a research assignment and IL instruction from their English Composition instructor as part of their regular coursework" (Mery, Newby, & Peng, 2012, p. 373).
Paraphrase:	A research article from 2012 discovered that students learn the least about information literacy on their own and from their English professors (Mery, Newby, & Peng, 2012, p. 373).
Summary:	Using a quasi-experimental method, with a control group that received no information literacy instruction and three treatment groups that received information literacy instruction from their English professor, or their librarian, or multiple instructions from their librarian, researchers discovered that students learned the least from their English professor, learned a little more than that without instruction, but did well with instruction from the librarian. They did best when receiving multiple instruction sessions from their librarian (Mery, Newby, & Peng, 2012).
2nd Article, with author in signal phrase	
Quotation:	In an extensive research project conducted by Booth, Lowe, Tagge, and Stone (2015), their evidence showed that "Simply put, the quantity of librarian engagement was a clear correlate to the quality of student learning" (p. 635).

Figure 10.5: Quotation Worksheet Example

Paraphrase:	Booth, Lowe, Tagge, and Stone (2015) discovered through their research that the more students engage with a librarian in their classes, the more they learn about information literacy (p. 365)
Summary:	The research study conducted by Booth, Lowe, Tagge, and Stone (2015) examined two factors, level of librarian engagement in the class and syllabus/ assignment design collaboration for information literacy, in first-year seminar courses. Student learning was evaluated by applying a scoring rubric to research papers and from student and faculty evaluations. Student achievement was highest when both the level of librarian engagement was high and the level of information literacy in the syllabus was high. This is a clear sign that librarians need to have high levels of involvement in instruction and syllabus/assignment design in courses. However, students and faculty were unaware of the amount of information that students learned, and did not see their actual level of achievement. This problem of perception is detrimental to the very collaboration that improved student performance.
Bibliography:	Booth, C., Lowe, M. S., Tagge, N., & Stone, S. M. (2015). Degrees of Impact: Analyzing the Effects of Progressive Librarian Course Collaborations on Student Performance. *College & Research Libraries*, 76(5), 623–651. http://doi.org/10.5860/crl.76.5.623 Mery, Y., Newby, J., & Peng, K. (2012). Why One-shot Information Literacy Sessions Are Not the Future of Instruction: A Case for Online Credit Courses. *College & Research Libraries*, 73(4), 366–377.

Figure 10.5: (*Continued*)

Citation Style:	
1st Article, without author in signal phrase	
Quotation:	
Paraphrase:	
Summary:	
2nd Article, with author in signal phrase	
Quotation:	
Paraphrase:	
Summary:	
Bibliography:	

Figure 10.6: Quotation Worksheet

CHAPTER 11

Evaluating Your Product and Communicating Your Results

In This Chapter

You will learn:

- How to organize your research paper
- How to use logic to support your hypothesis
- How to proofread your paper
- How to evaluate your research project
- How to communicate your results
- How to learn from this experience

Organization

The organization of your research project is very important. A well-organized paper is easier to write, read, and understand. Each section should flow into the next logically without harsh jumps in thoughts and ideas. This is why you need an outline. An outline will help you organize your thoughts and lay out the path you are going to follow from hypothesis through arguments to the conclusion. With an outline in place, you can organize your information and plan when you will mention which articles and ideas.

> **Typical Research Paper Outline**
>
> - Introduction
>   - State the problem and hypothesis
> - Literature Review
>   - Summary of relevant research
> - Methodology
>   - How the research is constructed
> - Findings
>   - Discussion of the results
> - Conclusions
>   - Meaning and impact on hypothesis

Figure 11.1: Typical Research Paper Outline

A typical research follows an outline like the one shown in Figure 11. The introduction is where the problem to be investigated is described. The hypothesis that will be tested as a means to solve the problem is stated in the introduction, also. The literature review and methodology were discussed in Chapter 6. The literature review serves to present the background and the current state of research for the topic at hand. It should also present the need for the current research.

The methodology section outlines exactly how the research was done. If you created a survey, you need to be specific about the intent of the survey, the audience for the survey, how you found people to take the survey, and how many completed surveys you received. You need to specify if you gathered quantitative data; measurable and numerical data that may be used to create numerical answers like percentages, likelihoods, and correlations; or qualitative data that describes how people feel about the subject or an aspect of it and can be used to create an overall impression of people's feelings about the topic. You need to explain how you processed this data to generate the numbers or impression you found, and you also need to explain any limitations your research methods may have regarding the outcome they can produce.

In the findings section, you discuss what your research found and what these results may indicate. This leads directly to your conclusion where you state what the results mean and how they support, prove, or disprove your hypothesis and how your results fit into or expand the knowledge of your field.

```
┌─────────────────────────────────────────┐
│              Basic Outline               │
│                                          │
│  ○ Introduction                          │
│     • State the problem and hypothesis   │
│  ○ Body                                  │
│     • Major points or                    │
│     • Stages or periods or               │
│     • Compare and contrast               │
│  ○ Conclusions                           │
│     • Meaning and impact on hypothesis   │
│                                          │
└─────────────────────────────────────────┘
```

Figure 11.2: Basic Outline

A more basic outline is illustrated in Figure 11.2. You always have the introduction and conclusion sections, and they contain the same information as before. The body of the outline is where you make your case, examine a few major themes of a work, review historical periods, stages of development, facets of a person's life, or compare and contrast two works.

Your outline should cover all the points you want to make and in a logical order, for example, building from least impactful to most impactful information. Your outline should stay focused on your hypothesis. Use your outline as your write with each bullet point in the outline a header in your research paper. This will help keep you on track and prevent you from going off on tangents that do not relate to the purpose of the paper. If you are writing your paper and you forgot an important point, fit it into the proper spot in your outline, first, then rearrange the sections of your paper to maintain a logical order. Microsoft Word, for example, makes it easy to drag and drop sections of a paper in the Navigation pane as long as headers are used for each section.

Logic

Logic is reasoning that follows scientific principles and uses facts to support the "validity of inference" (Merriam-Webster, Inc. 2016a). For example, the research done by Booth, Lowe, Tagge, and Stone found that while having one or two sessions with a library in a first-year seminar class was good, having more sessions and greater involvement by the librarian in the course showed a greater learning of information literacy skills (Booth, Lowe, Tagge, and Stone, 2015). This led them to the inference that more is better when it comes to information literacy instruction and integration. They supported that inference with evidence from their research and drew a logical conclusion.

Evaluate your reasoning as you write your paper. Start with the common sense test. Does your argument seem reasonable and make sense? Does B really follow A? For example, stating that global warming is leading to lower academic achievement among college students does not pass the test. Make sure that when you arrive at a conclusion, it is supported by evidence from your information sources, or your previous reasoning based on your information sources. When you include a quote or paraphrase in your research project, you should discuss how that information supports your reasoning and builds the case for your hypothesis. Your logic should be straightforward, easy to understand and stated in a clear, direct manner whether synthesizing the thoughts of others or stating original thoughts. Clear and direct logic based on your research and information sources gives validity to your arguments and to your research project.

Your logic should build on what came before it, and it should lay the groundwork for your next argument. This should all build to your conclusion, the final outcome of your research. Your conclusion links back to your hypothesis in the introduction of your paper. Your evidence and logic all build to proving this final, overarching statement of your research.

Proofreading

Proofreading is your last chance to correct mistakes in your research paper. It is the last evaluation before sending your work out into the world. There are two varieties of proofreading: content, and spelling and grammar. Evaluating your logic and reasoning is proofreading for content, so we will look at proofreading for spelling and grammar errors. While you should watch for these errors as you write your paper, proofreading as a formal process is done after you finish your paper. When proofreading your own work, you often lapse into reading for content and miss your spelling and grammar errors.

Word processors will help you find more spelling errors than you actually made but not all of your grammar errors by conveniently marking errors for you to review. The small squiggly lines used to mark these errors are easy to miss. You need to make sure you find them all. The spellcheckers in word processors mark every word they do not know. That includes not just your misspellings but also authors' names and words that are too new or too discipline-specific to be included in the dictionary. It is important to read carefully through your paper, find the marked words, decide if it is a true spelling error or a limitation of the word processor, and correct the errors.

While spellcheckers are great, they cannot tell you if you used the wrong word. Grammar checkers in word processors should be able to fill this void, but they miss many mistakes. In the examples given in Figure 11.3, each sentence has an obvious grammatical error. The grammar checker in two word processors did not find these mistakes. In the first example, a typing mistake results in a correctly spelled word that makes no sense in the sentence. The word should be "horses," but this type of word usage error is beyond the abilities of a basic grammar checker. So too is verb agreement with a compound subject. The second and third examples both have a compound subject. The verb should take the plural form. While Jim *is* happy, Bob and Jim *are* happy.

Add-in grammar checkers for your word processor do a much better job than word processors' grammar checkers. Grammarly (http://www.grammarly.com) and Ginger (http://www.gingersoftware.com/grammarcheck) both have a free version of their grammar checker that works within Word. One of them corrected the first two errors in our example, while the other corrected all three. They both find many errors that a word processor will miss. The paid versions of these programs offer more features to provide more help with your writing. If you need to check only one or two sentences, Grammar Check for Sentence (http://www.grammarcheckforsentence.com) will find your errors.

You cannot rely on spellcheckers and grammar checkers to find all of your mistakes. You still need to proofread your paper. One method of proofreading is to read your paper aloud. Hearing the words will

1. Wild hoses roam the Nevada high country.

2. Bob and Jim is happy.

3. The control group and the test group has the same demographics.

Figure 11.3: Grammar Errors

help you find sentences that are confusing. Another technique is to read each sentence in a paragraph backward. This isolates the words from their context making it easier to spot spelling errors. Finally, you can ask a friend to proofread your paper and you will return the favor for them. They will find more errors than you because they are not as well acquainted with the content as you are. An organized, well-reasoned paper that is free of spelling and grammatical errors will impress any instructor.

Communicating Your Findings

Part of the research process is communicating your findings with others. This is not a part of every information need. If you only wanted to know who that actress is in that movie, there is no need to communicate your findings. However, if you had a bet with your friend that actress is Lilian Gish in *Night of the Hunter*, then you know a lot about movies and you want to tell your friend how right you are.

Classroom Communication

Communicating your results is the most important part of the research process. We need to share our information so that others may learn from it and use it to discover new information. When we talk about communicating the results of your research project in this book, we are referring to two possible avenues of communication, classroom and professional. Classroom communication is as simple as submitting a paper to your instructor or talking to a classmate about what you learned. You may also have to do a presentation by yourself or as part of a group project to communicate your results to the class. This necessitates a medium other than writing.

The medium you use to communicate your results may be specified by your instructor or the choice may be left up to you. In either case, be sure to fit the information to the strengths of the medium. For example, if you interview veterans about their experiences, then a video or audio recording works better than a transcription. If you want to document an event, then photographs or a video recording does the job best. Mixed media, like combining your photographs with a written report, have the strengths of each medium to present your case. Creating a web page will allow you to use all the media mentioned in this paragraph. If you have a lot of data that you need to present in tables or charts, a paper or a PowerPoint presentation allows you to explain the meaning of your data. When using other media, be sure not to overwhelm your audience with too many photos or overly long videos. These can be just as dull as the written word.

Professional Communication

Professional communication is presenting your findings in a formal manner through a presentation at a conference or through publication. When you create a great research project, your instructor should encourage you to present it at a conference. Many colleges and universities hold a conference for their undergraduates to present their projects. A conference is a formal meeting where people who share the same interests present and discuss their research and views. The next steps up from a conference sponsored by your school are state conferences, national conferences, and international conferences. Typically, you need to apply to present at a conference. It is harder to get accepted to present at a national conference than a state conference because there is more competition, and it is harder still to get accepted at an international conference because of the bigger pool of applications. Presenting at a conference is prestigious and widens the audience for your work. It may also result in additional feedback about your research project and presentation that will help you with future projects and presentations.

A great research project should also be published. Your instructor may want to work with you to get your ideas published or may encourage you to do it alone. Your instructor should know of a number of journals that would be interested in your work. Otherwise, there is a list of journals dedicated to or that publish undergraduate and high school research. One such list is maintained by the Council on Undergraduate Research, a national organization, and includes a description of the journals, what they publish, and links to their websites (http://www.cur.org/resources/students/undergraduate_journals). Getting your article published is an honor and a feather in your cap when applying for colleges or graduate schools. As with presentation, it expands the audience for your research and will provide you with useful feedback. Presentations are wonderful, but they are ephemeral. Publications contribute to the scholarly process for years.

The Takeaway

In Chapter 10, we talked about part 2 of the Pathways model, which includes what you have learned. It is important to reflect upon this after you have completed your project. Reflect on what you learned about the research process in addition to what you learned about the subject of your research. Reflection helps synthesize the information you learned. The best way to reflect is to write down your thoughts in your words. Reflective writing is an exercise in critical thinking or metacognition, which means thinking about your thinking. It asks you to think about what you did and what you can do better, what you learned, how you came to know this, and what else you want to know.

In practical terms, start by thinking about the research process. How well did it go? What would you do differently next time? How would you improve your search? How would you find better quality information? How effective was your use of information? Did you cite your sources correctly? What could improve this aspect of your use of information?

Next, think about the subject of your research. Did you answer your initial question? Is your answer satisfactory, or could it be improved upon? What did you know about the topic before you began, and what do you know now? Did learning this information change your opinions on the topic? Did it increase your interest or leave you flat?

Answers to these questions will be personal. Maybe using a citation manager will help you keep track of your research better and improve your citations next time. Perhaps you need to realize when you are not finding good information, and you need to ask the librarian for help. This, in itself, is an important skill. Possibly a better outline will help you keep your paper focused. Maybe a more specific search statement or a subject database will lead to a better topic. Perhaps a more critical evaluation of the information found should be done before including it in a paper. When you answer these and other questions for yourself, you are taking control of your education and learning deeply.

While the purpose of this book is to teach you how to do these things better and more efficiently, there is something much bigger than this about the learning process. At the beginning of this book, we talked about how we are creatures of information. We are made from information. We create information, and we consume information. If we choose to, our minds can always be open to new information, and we can always be learning. When we learn something from the infor-mation we have gathered, it becomes part of who we are. It helps us grow and become better human beings. Information we consume and synthesize becomes knowledge. Knowledge changes who we are and who we want to become. Using the knowledge we have gained can change the world.

Vocabulary

arguments

classroom communication

conclusion

conference

evidence

grammar checker

inference

literature review

logic

medium

metacognition

methodology

organization

outline

professional communication

proofreading

qualitative data

quantitative data

reasoning

reflection

spellchecker

Questions for Reflection

Why should you evaluate your research process?

How does an outline impact a research paper?

What effect does an unsupported statement have on your research paper?

What does good reasoning look like?

Does reflection affect learning?

Assignment

Open your research journal and using the full Pathways model mark the route you took through your research process (Figures 11.4 and 11.5).

Next, reflecting upon your research process and using your Pathways, discuss your research process and what you learned about it by filling in the worksheet (Figures 11.6 and 11.7).

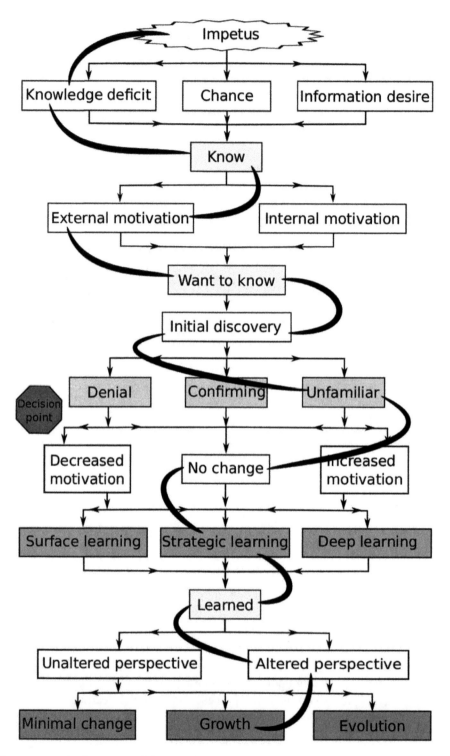

Figure 11.4: Pathways Model Example

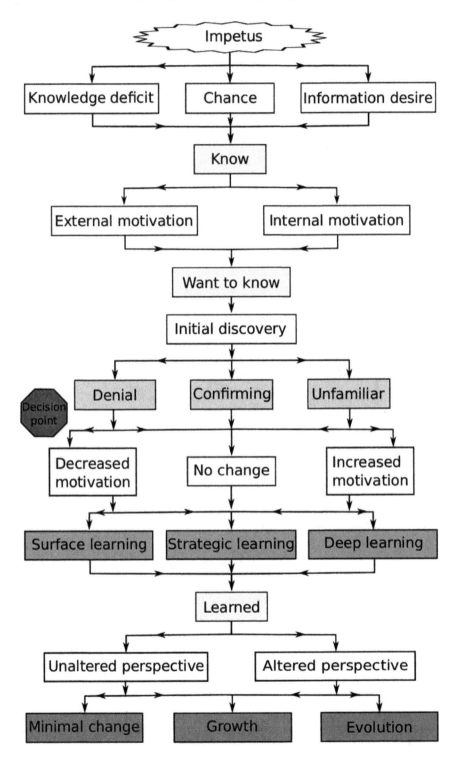

Figure 11.5: Pathways Information Seeking Model

Research Question:	I thought my research questions was pretty good, but it did not lead to a good search statement. I revised my question a few times with my search statements until I had a focused and specific question.
Search Statement:	My first search statement did not work well. I returned too many things and most were not relevant to my topic. I changed my search by adding an additional AND statement, plus I changed one of my keywords to a subject term. This search found a good amount of relevant information. I applied facets and that got me only full-text and scholarly articles. I think my search went well after these modifications. Next time, I would be less afraid to experiment with changes to my search statement.
Database Choice:	I used our standard, general database. I thought I might need to switch to a different database, but after changing my search and applying facets, I found plenty of good information, here. I would use this database, again, and only switch if I did not find enough information.
Evaluation of Information:	I evaluated articles for an earlier assignment. Using the facets was nice to limit the material to just scholarly journals. I did not want popular magazine articles. The evaluation criteria really helped me to pick good articles. I would be even more particular next time about the articles I picked. I would make sure they were very current and based on original research.

Figure 11.6: Research Reflection Worksheet Example

Pathways Model:	The Pathways model showed me that I was doing this because it was an assignment. I was not really interested in it. I thought I knew more about searching than I did, and I was unfamiliar with a lot of this stuff. My motivation didn't really change, but I did learn something new, and I know I am a better researcher, now.
What was Learned:	I learned that the research process takes practice to do well and that you should actually experiment and change your search up to make sure you are finding all the good information. There is no one perfect search. I learned that facets really help limit your results to the types of information you want, but that you still need to evaluate what you found to get the best stuff for your research project.

Figure 11.6: (*Continued*)

Research Question:	
Search Statement:	
Database Choice:	
Evaluation of Information:	
Pathways Model:	
What was Learned:	

Figure 11.7: Research Reflection Worksheet

References

American Association of School Librarians. 2007. "Standards for the 21st-Century Learner." Available at: http://www.ala.org/ala/mgrps/divs/aasl/guidelines andstandards/learningstandards/AASL_LearningStandards.pdf.

Birdsong, Lark, and Jennifer Freitas. 2012. "Helping the Non-Scholar Scholar: Information Literacy for Lifelong Learners." *Library Trends* 60 (3): 588–610.

Blundell, Shelley, and Frank Lambert. 2014. "Information Anxiety from the Undergraduate Student Perspective: A Pilot Study of Second-Semester Freshmen." *Journal of Education for Library & Information Science* 55 (4): 261–73.

"Boole, George." 2013. In *Computer Sciences*, 2nd ed., 2: 25–27. Software and Hardware, eds. K. Lee Lerner, and Brenda Wilmoth Lerner. Detroit: Macmillan Reference USA. Available at: http://go.galegroup.com/ps/i.do?id=GALE% 7CCX2761000092&v=2.1&u=sutahu&it=r&p=GVRL&sw=w&asid= 2a5f81bfb6201834f23aea5bde4a990b.

Booth, Char, M. Sara Lowe, Natalie Tagge, and Sean M. Stone. 2015. "Degrees of Impact: Analyzing the Effects of Progressive Librarian Course Collaborations on Student Performance." *College & Research Libraries* 76 (5): 623–51. doi:10.5860/crl.76.5.623.

Bruce, Christine Susan. 1999. "Workplace Experiences of Information Literacy." *International Journal of Information Management* 19 (1): 33.

"Bureau of Labor Statistics Data." 2016. Available at: http://data.bls.gov/timeseries/ CUUR0000SA0?output_view=pct_12mths. Accessed May 26.

Cheuk, Bonnie. 2008. "Delivering Business Value through Information Literacy in the Workplace." *Libri: International Journal of Libraries & Information Services* 58 (3): 137–43.

"Chicago School of Economics." 2016. *Wikipedia, the Free Encyclopedia.* Available at: https://en.wikipedia.org/w/index.php?title=Chicago_school_of_economics& oldid=725261974.

"Cold Fusion." 2016. *Wikipedia, the Free Encyclopedia.* Available at: https://en.wiki pedia.org/w/index.php?title=Cold_fusion&oldid=722578972.

Creative Commons. 2016. "About The Licenses." Available at: http://creativecommons .org/licenses/. Accessed May 11.

Darity, William A., Jr., ed. 2008. "Cognitive Dissonance." In *International Encyclopedia of the Social Sciences*, 2nd ed., 1: 599–601. Detroit: Macmillan Reference USA. Available at: http://go.galegroup.com/ps/i.do?id=GALE%7CCX 3045300374&v=2.1&u=sutahu&it=r&p=GVRL&sw=w&asid=5492ee 183696a742163295ca4a5b9464.

Dawkins, Richard. 1986. *The Blind Watchmaker*. 1st American ed. New York: Norton.

Elkind, David. 2002. "Piaget, Jean (1896–1980)." In *Encyclopedia of Education*, ed. James W. Guthrie, 2nd ed., 5: 1894–98. New York: Macmillan Reference USA. Available at: http://go.galegroup.com/ps/i.do?id=GALE%7CCX340320 0491&v=2.1&u=sutahu&it=r&p=GVRL&sw=w&asid=693513378074624cb7 25ff580650ddf4.

Elsevier B.V. 2016a. "Product Detail: Brain Research." Available at: http://www .myelsevier.com/browse/product_details.jsp?productId=ELS_AG_BS-PRD- 05018.

Elsevier B.V. 2016b. "Product Detail: International Journal of Radiation Oncology / Biology / Physics." Available at: http://www.myelsevier.com/browse/ product_details.jsp?productId=ELS_AG_BS-PRD-07551.

Fishman, Stephen. 2008. *The Public Domain: How to Find and Use Copyright-Free Writings, Music, Art & More*. 4th ed. Berkeley, CA: Nolo.

Foundation for Critical Thinking. 1997. *Critical Thinking; Basic Theory and Instructional Structures*. Wye Mills, MD: Foundation for Critical Thinking.

Gleick, James. 2011. *The Information: A History, a Theory, a Flood*. 1st ed. New York: Pantheon Books.

Goldhaber, Dale E. 2002. "Theories of Development." In *Child Development*, ed. Neil J. Salkind, 413–17. New York: Macmillan Reference USA. http:// go.galegroup.com/ps/i.do?id=GALE%7CCX3401000280&v=2.1&u= sutahu&it=r&p=GVRL&sw=w&asid=2ed4bba54709957cca7002e24 c9e5eb3.

Griffin, Darrin J., San Bolkan, and Alan K. Goodboy. 2015. "Academic Dishonesty beyond Cheating and Plagiarism: Students' Interpersonal Deception in the College Classroom." *Qualitative Research Reports in Communication* 16 (1): 9–19. doi:10.1080/17459435.2015.1086416.

Gross, Melissa, and Don Latham. 2007. "Attaining Information Literacy: An Investigation of the Relationship between Skill Level, Self-Estimates of Skill, and Library Anxiety." *Library & Information Science Research (07408188)* 29 (3): 332–53. doi:10.1016/j.lisr.2007.04.012.

"Guidelines on Open Access to Scientific Publications and Research Data in Horizon 2020." 2016. EUROPEAN COMMISSION Directorate—General for Research & Innovation. Available at: http://ec.europa.eu/research/partici pants/data/ref/h2020/grants_manual/hi/oa_pilot/h2020-hi-oa-pilot-guide_ en.pdf.

Head, Alison J. 2013. "Project Information Literacy: What Can Be Learned about the Information-Seeking Behavior of Today's College Students?" In *Imagine, Innovate, Inspire: The Proceedings of the ACRL 2013 Conference*,

ed. Dawn M. Mueller, 472–82. Chicago: ALA. Available at: http://www.ala
.org/acrl/sites/ala.org.acrl/files/content/conferences/confsandpreconfs/2013/
papers/Head_Project.pdf.

"How Google Search Works—Search Console Help." 2016. Available at: https://
support.google.com/webmasters/answer/70897?hl=en. Accessed June 21.

"Information." 2003. *McGraw-Hill Dictionary of Scientific and Technical Terms*, 6th ed.
New York: McGraw-Hill.

InfoSpace. 2016. "About Dogpile." Available at: http://www.dogpile.com/dogpiletestC/
support/aboutus.

"Isaac Newton." 2016. *Wikiquote*. Available at: https://en.wikiquote.org/wiki/Isaac_
Newton. Accessed June 16.

"Library of Congress Classification." 2016. *Wikipedia, the Free Encyclopedia*. Available at: https://en.wikipedia.org/w/index.php?title=Library_of_Congress_
Classification&oldid=724592597.

"Literate." 2016. *OED Online*. Oxford University Press. Accessed May 25. Available
at: http://www.oed.com.proxy.li.suu.edu:2048/view/Entry/109070.

"Mariana Trench." 2016. *Wikipedia, the Free Encyclopedia*. Available at: https://
en.wikipedia.org/w/index.php?title=Mariana_Trench&oldid=721951445.

Martin, Jonathan. 2014. "Plagiarism Costs Degree for Senator John Walsh." *The New
York Times*, October 10. Available at: http://www.nytimes.com/2014/10/11/
us/politics/plagiarism-costs-degree-for-senator-john-walsh.html.

McBrien, J. Lynn and Ronald S. Brandt. 1997. *The Language of Learning: A Guide to
Education Terms*. Alexandria, VA: Association for Supervision and Curriculum Development.

Mellon, Constance A. 2015. "Library Anxiety: A Grounded Theory and Its Development." *College & Research Libraries* 76 (3): 276–82. doi:10.5860/crl.76.
3.276.

Merriam-Webster, Inc. 2015. "Humanities." Available at: http://www.merriam-
webster.com/dictionary/humanities.

Merriam-Webster, Inc. 2016a. "Definition of Logic." Available at: http://www
.merriam-webster.com/dictionary/logic. Accessed July 12.

Merriam-Webster, Inc. 2016b. "Definition of Primary." Available at: http://www
.merriam-webster.com/dictionary/primary. Accessed June 2.

Middle States Commission on Higher Education. 2014. "Standard for Accreditation
and Requirements of Affiliation." Middle States Commission on Higher
Education. Available at: http://www.msche.org/publications_view.asp?id
PublicationType=1&txtPublicationType=Standards+for+Accreditation+
and+Requirements+of+Affiliation.

Mueller, Pam A., and Daniel M. Oppenheimer. 2014. "The Pen Is Mightier Than the
Keyboard Advantages of Longhand Over Laptop Note Taking." *Psychological Science* 25 (6): 1159–68. doi:10.1177/0956797614524581.

"NIH Public Access Policy." 2015. *Wikipedia, the Free Encyclopedia*. Available at:
https://en.wikipedia.org/w/index.php?title=NIH_Public_Access_Policy&
oldid=686699752.

"1960 Valdivia Earthquake." 2016. *Wikipedia, the Free Encyclopedia*. Available at:
https://en.wikipedia.org/w/index.php?title=1960_Valdivia_earthquake&
oldid=722059152.

O'Sullivan, Carmel. 2002. "Is Information Literacy Relevant in the Real World?" *Reference Services Review* 30 (1): 7–14.

Petress, Ken. 2004. "Critical Thinking: An Extended Definition." *Education (Chula Vista, Calif.)* 124 (3): 461–66.

Project Information Literacy. 2016a. "Home." June 24. Available at: http://project infolit.org/.

Project Information Literacy. 2016b. "PIL Research." Available at: http://projectinfolit .org/images/img/pilresearchiglarge.png. Accessed July 15.

Riddell, Thelma. 2007. "Critical Assumptions: Thinking Critically about Critical Thinking." *Journal of Nursing Education* 46 (3): 121–26.

Ridpath, Ian. 2012. "Mars." *A Dictionary of Astronomy.* Oxford University Press. Available at: http://www.oxfordreference.com/view/10.1093/acref/9780 199609055.001.0001/acref-9780199609055-e-2273.

Shapiro, Jeremy J., and Shelley K. Hughes. 1996. "Information Literacy as a Liberal Art." *Educom Review* 31 (2): 31.

Sharp, Tim. 2012. "What Is the Temperature of Mars?" *Space.com.* Available at: http:// www.space.com/16907-what-is-the-temperature-of-mars.html.

"Standards (Effective July 1, 2016)." 2016. *Colleges & Universities (CIHE)/ Commission on Institutions of Higher Education.* February 4. Available at: https://cihe.neasc.org/standards-policies/standards-accreditation/standards-effective-july-1-2016.

Stebbins, Michael. 2013. "Expanding Public Access to the Results of Federally Funded Research." *Whitehouse.gov.* February 22. Available at: https://www .whitehouse.gov/blog/2013/02/22/expanding-public-access-results-federally-funded-research.

Tavani, Herman. 2014. "Search Engines and Ethics." In *The Stanford Encyclopedia of Philosophy*, ed. Edward N. Zalta, Spring 2014. Available at: http://plato .stanford.edu/archives/spr2014/entries/ethics-search/.

UNESCO. 2003. "The Prague Declaration: Towards an Information Literate Society." 20–23. Available at: http://portal.unesco.org/ci/en/ev.php-URL_ ID=19636&URL_DO=DO_TOPIC&URL_SECTION=201.html.

The University of Chicago. 2016. "Nobel Laureates." *The University of Chicago.* Available at: http://www.uchicago.edu/about/accolades/22/. Accessed June 15.

U.S. Copyright Office. 2012. "Copyright Basics." United States Copyright Office. Available at: http://www.copyright.gov/circs/circ1.pdf.

U.S. Copyright Office. 2016. "More Information on Fair Use." March. Available at: http://www.copyright.gov/fair-use/more-info.html.

U.S. Department of Commerce, NOAA. 2016. "The Planet Mars." Available at: http:// www.weather.gov/fsd/mars. Accessed June 15.

USA.Gov. 2016. "U.S. Government Works." Available at: https://www.usa.gov/ government-works. Accessed July 8.

World Intellectual Property Organization. 2016. "What Is Intellectual Property?" *World Intellectual Property Organization.* Available at: http://www.wipo .int/about-ip/en/. Accessed July 6.

WorldWideWebSize.com. 2016. "The Size of the World Wide Web (The Internet)." June 5. Available at: http://www.worldwidewebsize.com/.

Index

About the Author

Scott Lanning received his Master of Library Science from Northern Illinois University. He has been a reference librarian throughout his long career, providing library instruction to students as part of his jobs. He currently teaches reference services and information literacy courses at Southern Utah University. Scott is also the author of *Reference and Instructional Services for Information Literacy Skills in School,* which is now in its third edition.